Moving Heaven & Earth

Moving Heaven & Earth

A Personal Journey into International Adoption

by BARBARA U. BIRDSEY

with George Cadwalader

THE *F*RANCIS PRESS

WASHINGTON, D.C.

Printed in the United States of America

FIRST EDITION

LIBRARY OF CONGRESS CATALOGING-IN-PUBLICATION DATA

Birdsey, Barbara U., 1944–
    Moving heaven & earth : a personal journey into international adoption / by Barbara U. Birdsey with George Cadwalader.
        p.   cm.
    Includes bibliographical references.
    ISBN 0-9665051-3-1 (hardcover)
        1. Birdsey, Barbara U., 1944– 2. Adoptive parents—Massachusetts—Biography. 3. Intercountry adoption—Central America. 4. Intercountry adoption—Massachusetts. I. Title: Moving heaven and earth. II. Cadwalader, George, 1939–   III. Title.

    HV874.82.B57 A3 2000
    362.73'4'092—dc21   [B]   00-057812

Book design by Christopher Kuntze

Published by The Francis Press
Washington, D.C.

*This book is dedicated to
my three wonderful children
and my patient husband.*

Contents

Foreword

$\mathcal{A}$ T a time when there has never been a greater interest in international adoption, Barbara Birdsey's book is opportune. Although the events of her story took place in the 1980s, the lessons to be learned are still timely. Many countries with adoption programs have made progress in establishing regulations, but it is still necessary to be cautious.

This book is written from the heart of a woman who wants to make a better life for children in a world that makes this difficult to do—a world that too often wants to benefit financially from the needs of children and the anxiousness of people who want to have children. Barbara Birdsey, properly, puts the needs of children first while also understanding well the potential parents' longing to nurture a child. Determined to avoid the pitfalls of large organizations, Barbara kept her agency small. She was devoted to providing quality care to waiting children and parents who had to contend with endless bureaucracies and long periods of uncertainty.

Once prospective adoptive parents have reached the decision to fulfill their desire to parent through adoption, their lives become consumed with accomplishing their goal. First, there is the anxiety about the home study and approval process. Then there is the seemingly never-ending gathering of documents, the notarization and authentication, and the expense. Finally, there are no more tasks for the family, and the wait for a referral of a child begins. Once a referral is accepted, they wait to travel. Each of these periods requires "hand holding" on the part of the agency. This is not possible in a large agency with workers with large caseloads.

I have known Barbara Birdsey since the mid-1970s, when we both worked at a residential facility for emotionally disturbed and mildly retarded children on Cape Cod. Barbara went on to develop her own international agency, and I joined a well-known adoption agency in Boston. I am now an adoption specialist at The Home for Little Wanderers, a human-service agency with international and domestic adoption programs.

Today, just as when Barbara was active in the field, one must still be vigilant when planning an international adoption and choosing an agency. The intercountry pact known as the Hague Convention, however, offers real hope for improvement. When ratified by the nations that participated in the 1993 meeting, the Hague Convention will create the legal framework for safeguarding thousands of needy children throughout the world and the families who seek to adopt them. It is difficult to project, however, when worldwide standards of service will be established. While some countries—Bolivia, for example—need only the signature of the head of government to ratify the Convention, the United States requires full congressional approval. At the present time, the final legislation is being considered by both the Senate and House of Representatives.

In the meantime, Barbara's humorous and insightful tale is here to help us understand the joys and perils of international adoption.

Marilyn W. Sneden
BOSTON, MASSACHUSETTS

Preface

WHEN I embarked on my journey into the strange world of international adoptions, I did so with only the vaguest notion of what I was getting into. At the beginning, in 1980, my husband, David, and I were simply hoping to add a new member to our family. The frustrations of that quest, though it was ultimately successful, convinced me that there had to be a better way. And so I founded an international adoption agency to find homes in the United States for destitute children from Central America and the Philippines. Close encounters with some sleazy operators later compelled me to take on a third role: as victims' advocate. In all, I devoted ten intensely emotional and, in the end, highly rewarding years to international adoption. Plus I had experiences that most people never have.

Many adoptive parents just pack away their feelings and lose themselves in their "finally" adopted child, but I needed to put my experiences on paper to sort out what they meant for me . . . and for others considering adopting children overseas. I felt certain my story could be useful to people who were as ill-prepared as I had been. I also believed I had a debt to repay. I was not one of those people who thought, "I've got my baby, I don't care what else happens." I did care. Nothing was harder for me to swallow than that some people didn't care: the mindless bureaucrat telling me something could not be done, the incompetent social worker, the greedy entrepreneur. These kids, their birth parents, and the people who wanted to adopt them deserved better.

If the book was to be helpful, I knew it had to be interesting and enjoyable to read. It needed to capture the personalities, drama, and pathos I had encountered. I realized that my narrative skills were sadly deficient and I would need help. I turned to George Cadwalader, a man I had known for a number of years as the founder and director of a school for delinquent teenagers on a remote Massachusetts island. He had the ability to cut through the outer layers of a subject and get right to the core, to tell it like it was, to get things accomplished, and always with a sense of humor. George had recently written a marvelous book about his experience running the school. Called *Castaways,* it dealt with tough, real-life issues in a style at once amusing, moving, and instructive. This was just the sort of approach I thought was needed for my story. George agreed to help. After trying out different strategies, we ultimately decided that I would recount my rambling, confused story to him in a series of interviews. He would take detailed notes, ask questions, then try to make sense of it in a manuscript. The narrative that emerged was remarkably faithful to my memories of those eventful years. George understood me and where I was coming from. He also got to know the characters he had never met and to think the way they thought.

When the manuscript was finished in 1991, we made a half-hearted attempt to find a publisher. None rushed to seize upon the opportunity, so we each went on to other things. I was pleased when George wrote me last year to say that a long-time friend of his had recently started a publishing company called The Francis Press that specialized in biographies and memoirs. He thought it might be interested in my story.

This book could never have happened without George. I am extremely grateful to him for taking the responsibility of writing it so much to heart and for applying the same skills to my story as he did to his own.

I also want to thank Scotty and Nancy, "Sandy," "Juanita," and

"Lucinda" for sharing the work, the pain, the frustrations, and the happy endings that are part and parcel of this work. To "Mike Anderson," I am grateful for listening to our concerns and taking action. His integrity and perseverence meant a lot. Cherie and Dan Dryz had the courage to be our first guinea pigs in the business. They let us know they would be okay with whatever happened, and that made it possible for us to move ahead. I want to recognize and thank *all* those courageous people—parents adopting children and those giving up children for adoption—who in their private individual actions have demonstrated their faith in the process and have thus made important contributions to the building of families throughout the world.

I appreciate the advice and information from international adoption experts, in particular Betty Laning, and, even more recently, updates from Phyllis Loewenstein, and Marilyn Sneden. Finally, my husband and our three children supported me throughout, putting up with me through all the ups and downs.

As protection for some of the characters and for myself, many of the identifying features of the events described, such as names, locations, personal information, and circumstances, have been changed. The conversations and issues, however, remain true to the best of my ability.

Moving Heaven & Earth

1

The little boy in 19

_M_AY 1987. Eastern Airlines' night flight from Miami to Guatemala City was nearly empty. I sat at the rear of the tourist section. Two seats ahead of the lavatories was not the most pleasant place to be in a 727 flying through unstable tropical air, but I'd once seen a picture of an airliner's broken-off tail section sitting primly intact behind a burned-out fuselage, and ever since I'd always sat in the back.

I watched out my window as the lights of the Florida coast faded into the darkness of the ocean below. God, how I hated these flights! Endless hours in airplanes had not factored into my dreams three years earlier when I had committed myself to finding homes for orphaned Central American children. Meeting the families who would come to me in search of a child, cradling in my arms the solemn-faced little brown-eyed waifs for whom I might find a home, uniting abandoned children with the couples who could give them the love they needed—that had been my dream. But flying was the pits.

I'd invented a game to pass the time on airplanes. I called it "Peg the Passenger," and the object was to make up biographies for my fellow travelers. For example, the hawk-faced man with the thin tie who had helped me get my bag into the overhead locker: That one, I decided, had to be CIA. Then there were the three well-scrubbed, sandy-haired kids wearing chinos. Those would be missionaries. Their Bible Belt accents confirmed it. Add in some American businessmen in cotton suits, a party of wealthy Guatemalans returning from a Florida shopping trip, a few tourists, a Catholic priest. The usual. No, not quite the usual. Way up at the other end of the tourist section I spotted a Kekchi Indian woman, dressed in the voluminous tie-dyed skirt of her tribe. What had *she* been doing in Miami?

A balding head surrounded by a fringe of brown hair leaned out into the aisle four seats ahead and then disappeared again. I grinned. That one I would have pegged as Friar Tuck if I didn't know better. That one was James S. McTaggart, a/k/a Scotty, ex-priest, ex-community organizer, veteran of 20 years in the mountains of Central America, now my partner in the firm of Hermandad de Guadalupe, Adoption Agency. A man of many dimensions. Also many eccentricities, one of which was that he would never sit next to me on any form of public transportation. We were the best of friends. Together we had traveled countless miles, shared primitive accommodations, been sick from the same bad food, labored side by side over the innards of ancient vehicles, and talked our way through hostile military checkpoints. But as soon as we climbed onto a bus or plane, we became strangers. Whichever end I sat in, Scotty always went to the other.

The flight droned on. I tried to sleep but couldn't. A group ahead of me were into their third round of drinks and getting rowdy. Bankers, I figured, drowning their sorrows over the loans they'd just a few years before so cheerfully urged on any Latino who could sign his name. No, I decided, that wouldn't be right. Bankers, even bankrupt bankers, would still be up in first class.

One of the party-goers came unsteadily down the aisle and disappeared into the lavatory behind me. Fifteen minutes passed and I noticed drowsily that he hadn't come back out. Two more came noisily past my seat. "Ol' Lester must be in there huggin' the bucket!" one of them laughed as he went by.

"Ol' Lester was feelin' no pain!" agreed the other.

Ol' Lester was tying up the facilities. One of his friends stumbled into the unoccupied lavatory, and the other waited impatiently in the aisle.

The 727 hit turbulence and the "fasten seat belt sign" flashed on. The priest one seat ahead and across from where I sat didn't seem to notice. I wondered if I should say something to him. I thought perhaps he couldn't read English. No, it wasn't that. Right below the English edition was another warning. "*Aseguren sus cinturones.*" Surely he could read that. I noticed with a shock that he was missing half an ear.

The plane took a particularly violent lurch. The American in the aisle fell heavily against the priest's seat. I watched the cleric with half an ear turn silently and fix the apologizing gringo with an expression of such naked loathing that the man recoiled as if he had been hit. But he was too drunk to back off. "Hey!" he said, "cool your jets there, Padre! Look, I said I was sorry. Right? I mean . . . "

He faltered and fell silent. Ol' Lester, looking green, chose that moment to come staggering out of the lavatory. His friend tore free of the priest's mesmerizing glare and bolted for the open door. His eyes met mine as he went by. "Jesus!" he muttered, " what's that guy so worked up about?"

I could have told him. I remembered another Latino priest who had branded me the Devil's agent. That one was a barely literate backcountry pastor who had hated me as he hated all apostles of social change, especially if they were women. The radical Catholics at the other end of the theological spectrum weren't always much friendlier. Some had been willing to help me. Most had not been able to see beyond the rabid anti-Americanism that was a tenet of their revolutionary theology.

I pegged the cleric in the seat ahead of me as one of those gringo-haters. I wondered if he had lost that ear to an interrogator trained by that hawk-faced man with the thin tie. But I still found it hard to accept that anyone, particularly a priest, could hate me just for being an American. I decided to say nothing about the seat belt.

Lightning streaked across the sky and rain streaked across my window. The cabin speakers crackled into life. "Ahh. . ." drawled the captain with the kind of studied nonchalance that they must teach in flight school, "we got a little . . . ahhhhhhh . . . *weather* up ahead of us, folks.

Gonna be a little . . . ahhhhhhhhh . . . *bumpy* for a couple o' minutes so we're gonna ask that you remain seated with your seat belts fastened until we turn the light off. Gonna make us a little . . . ahhhhhhhhhhh . . . late getting into Guatemala International. Fifteen minutes maybe. Maybe a little longer. Just depends how long it takes to get around this mess. Okay?"

Although I was certainly not the model of timeliness, I hated planes being late. The legacy from my German ancestry, perhaps. I hated shifting gears. This morning I'd been a super-organized working mother in Cape Cod, Massachusetts. Tonight I would be in the land of endless *mañanas*. I hoped José, waiting for us at the airport, wouldn't mind. Our liaison with the local government authorities, José, was used to waiting.

José was a construction contractor. A tall, dignified man, he was the cousin of Juanita, the schoolteacher who was the next door neighbor of Pepe, the truck driver. All friends. All part of the network Scotty had put together to find adoptable children in Guatemala.

My mind drifted to the two Connecticut families whose hopes rode on the success of this trip I was making on their behalf. They were two very different families, who shared only the desperate longing for a child of their own. The Partridges were sweet, young farmers from northern Connecticut. The Warberg-Joneses were a pair of upper-middle-class professionals with a pack of advanced degrees, a hyphenated last name, and a restored colonial house near New Haven.

I knew what those four people were going through now. My husband, David, and I had experienced the same hopes and fears and doubts when we decided to adopt a child. We too had done battle with a host of state and federal bureaucrats. We had been burnt financially by agencies that hadn't delivered. We had faced the same bewilderment at finding so many people evidently bent on throwing obstructions in the way of something we knew was good. My mind drifted back to those frustrating, unhappy times.

A flight attendant telling me to straighten my seat pulled me back into the present. We were getting ready to land. Lester and his decidedly worse-for-wear friends were stirring groggily. Half-Ear, I noticed with a grin, had at some point during my revery conceded to temporal authority and fastened his seat belt.

The plane banked into a tight left turn over the city. It had been daylight the last time I arrived here. Tonight I could not see the volcanoes rising dramatically on the horizon, nor the broad, statue-lined Avenida de las Americas aimed like an arrow into the heart of the city, nor the little thread of highway we would soon be traveling east through the mountains to San Félix. Tonight I could see only lights. But I knew everything would be as I remembered it. Nothing ever changed in Guatemala City. A few more potholes, maybe, but everything else was the same. I had a sense of time unwinding, of history thrown into reverse. I knew that the people who had built those broad avenues must have had dreams. I knew they must have had some sense of future. But no more. Dreams were dead in Guatemala City. In my mind's eye, I could picture the statues along the Avenida in some not-too-distant time buried under the same vines that had buried the ruins of the Mayans.

I felt a jolt, heard the screech of rubber on tarmac, braced against the decelerating engines, and checked my watch: 10:00 p.m. local time. It would be midnight at home. David and our little Salvadorean daughter, Tamsin, would be fast asleep. My own day was just beginning.

Thin Tie helped me get my bag down. I thanked him and the two of us walked together down the ramp toward Immigrations. I stopped to fish my passport out of my handbag, and when I looked up Thin Tie had vanished.

Scotty, friend again now that we had landed, showed up at my elbow. "Who was that guy?" he asked.

"I haven't any idea. An unknown gentleman kind enough to help me with my bag. That's all I know about him."

"Gentleman, hell. You mean a spook. That guy had CIA written all over him."

Scotty was paranoid about spooks. When I first met him outside a hotel in El Salvador, his first question to me had been if I worked for the CIA. I smiled at that memory, then wondered if I too wasn't getting a bit paranoid on the same subject. Thin Tie probably sold vacuum cleaners.

The immigrations official was nice. *"Bienvenidos a Guatemala, señora,"* he smiled. *"Quantos dias va Usted quedarse acá?"*

"Cerca de una semana," I told him. One week more or less. I would like to have said "Until I find two children to take home with me," but I knew better.

Customs was next. Chaotic as always. I watched a deferential official pass the wealthy shoppers from first class quickly through a separate line and waited patiently while a less deferential agent tore apart the poor Kekchi Indian woman's many string-tied bags. Scotty, unable as always to contain his impatience with bureaucrats, raced back and forth from line to line. "Over here, Barbara!" he'd call. "This one's shorter!" and I'd pick up all my things and move. But Scotty's calls were invariably bad. The line I left always moved faster than the one he chose. So finally I gave it up. "No more," I said firmly. "I'm staying right here!"

My partner struck a martial pose. "I propose," he intoned, "to fight it out on this line if it takes all summer!"

"Who said that?"

"Ulysses S. Grant."

"Ulysses S. Grant," I told him, "would have understood how to get through Guatemalan customs!"

The line crawled forward, Scotty fidgeting, me resigned. I understood the ritual. Form here was more important than substance. As long as bags were duly searched and documents duly stamped, then officialdom could turn a blind eye to the trade in drugs and guns that knew no borders in this part of the world.

I looked in vain for José among the crowd waiting in the International Arrivals section on the other side of the glass partition. Then it was my turn with Customs. The inspector recognized me. Sometimes there were advantages to being tall and blond. "Welcome back, Señora. . ." he glanced at my papers. "Señora Birdzay. You are bringing more duty-free materials for . . . for the school. Yes?" He winked knowingly.

"But it *is* for the school!" I said indignantly. "The Baldwin School in San Félix. . . ."

"Of course, Señora. Radios and electronic calculators for the Baldwin School in San Félix."

"Listen, it is. . . ." Scotty nudged me and said something to the inspector in Spanish, too fast for me to catch. The man grinned, stamped our papers, and we were through.

José met us at the door. With me he was courtly and polite. With Scotty it was as if he had found a long lost brother. The two men rushed into a mighty, laughing *abrazo* and then stood holding each other by the arms, pouring out torrents of Spanish, while I waited, watching in wonder as Scotty the gringo metamorphosed into Scotty the Latino. It made me feel very much the outsider.

I knew I could never be a part of these exchanges, and I knew that it was more than simply a problem of language or of being a woman. I was part of a different world. Scotty had made the jump. But I would always be a gringo.

José and Scotty finally broke off, embarrassed at having forgotten me. José led the way apologetically to his car. It was not his car, actually, he explained. He had borrowed it from a friend. A friend who would be desolate if Scotty and I didn't stop by for a *cafecito*. "But isn't it too late to stop by tonight?" I protested.

"My friend expects us," said José. Scotty gave me a meaningful look, and I said no more. So we drove to the friend's apartment, where the ritual of *abrazos* and "How's the family, how's the dog" was repeated while I fought to stay awake until the coffee kicked in.

An hour later, after another round of *abrazos* and long farewells, I was wide awake and we were back in the car driving across the plaza toward the Presidential Palace. José was telling me that he had found a new lawyer with influence enough to move adoption papers rapidly through the courts, whom he wanted me to meet. But that, of course, would mean spending the night in the city.

I didn't argue. The coffee was wearing off and I no longer cared where I spent the night, as long as I could get some sleep. But it was not to be. Scotty wanted a pizza. So I drank more coffee while Scotty ate his pizza and José rhapsodized about the new lawyer's many connections in the highest levels of government. He talked about papers: which ones were needed, where to get them, who to sign them, who to stamp them, how to move them from one office to another.

José was fascinated with the flow of papers. I reminded him, more sharply than I had intended, that each one of those papers had a child's future attached to it. He looked at me in surprise. "You don't have to tell me that, Barbara," he said simply, and then continued with his dissertation about moving papers.

I felt myself getting lightheaded, pulled between the imperative to act and the temptation to float along timelessly in this ancient society. Who, I wondered, was being naive here? Me trying to rescue two out of Guatemala's two-hundred-thousand abandoned children? Or José with his faith in the power of papers? I was too tired to try to figure it out. Scotty looked at me and laughed. "Looks to me," he said through a mouth full of pizza, " that it's time you were in bed."

"It's about five hours *past* time I was in bed," I yawned.

"You wait here. I'll go get us rooms."

"Why don't I go with you?"

"No. Best you wait."

He was back in five minutes. "All set," he grinned. "Three bucks a room. If you'd been with me, my blond gringo lass, we'd have paid ten!"

José left us at the hotel lobby. I went to my room and Scotty to his. Before we parted, he took me by the arm. "Something's wrong, Barbara," he said. "I get the feeling José is a lot more pessimistic about our chances than he's letting on."

Whether it was because of the coffee or Scotty's warning, I couldn't sleep. So I spent what little was left of the night tossing in a none-too-clean bed and thinking about my two companions and the strange convergence of fates that had led the three of us to come together in a common cause.

Of the two men, I knew Scotty much better. Our paths had first crossed years before in San Salvador. He appeared out of the blue, a balding, round-faced, twinkly-eyed leprechaun, who'd jumped out of his car to order me back into my hotel on the grounds that I was in danger standing alone on the street. I'd taken him then as some kind of a nut, but he reappeared later that day, still concerned for my safety in that war-torn land. We went together to the hotel bar and talked for hours—he of his years as a priest and community organizer in Central America and I of my hopes to adopt a Salvadorean child—and when he left late that night bound for some distant Indian village the seeds of a lasting friendship and also (unbeknownst to either of us at the time) of our partnership had been sown.

Scotty recruited José as someone uniquely capable of breaking the logjams that were so much a part of doing business with Central American bureaucracies. Slim, greying, and very much the embodiment of his Spanish ancestors, José stood half a head taller than most of his countrymen, and, as I lay there thinking about this good-natured and endlessly patient man, I wondered how much his exceptional height and bearing contributed to his effectiveness at securing the cooperation of the various *funcionarios* who orchestrated the labyrinthian process of clearing children for adoption.

And then as dawn broke, I finally dropped off to sleep, taking some comfort in the thought that if the Leprechaun and the Patrician together couldn't get us the children we had come for, then probably it just couldn't be done.

*   *   *

The new lawyer's office, when the three of us arrived there the next morning, was all chrome and glass. Quite different from the dark, silent, wood-paneled chambers I'd come to associate with the legal profession in Guatemala. Good, I thought, maybe more modern decor reflects a more modern commitment to actually getting something done.

The man himself was short, plump, impeccably tailored, and, I suspected, a little bit vain. His intelligent, dark eyes took our measure as José introduced us. "And how," he asked, "might I be honored to assist the señora?"

Scotty answered for me. "You could help us and a lot of children if you could get us your government's approval for our agency to arrange adoptions from your publicly run orphanages."

"I see. The papers have been submitted?"

"Four years ago!"

"Four years? And what have you been doing in the meantime? Private adoptions?"

"Right!" I said. "For four years we've been turning away families who could have provided good homes to the children in your government's orphanages. With each child we place, we've been forced to go through the local courts to obtain approval for the surrender by the natural mother of her child. It's slow and it's painful. It's. . ."

I was off and running. The lawyer cleared his throat. "Of course," he said smoothly. "I understand entirely, and I can assure you that I share your impatience with our bureaucracy. It is such a shame. . . . So much suffering. . . . So many children. . . ."

I sensed a bit of theater in the way his eyes strayed to the pictures of his own children on the wall next to his desk. I noticed his long, slender fingers, and I pictured him at a piano in some elegant Spanish hacienda with a beautiful wife beside him and those smiling children at his feet. How often, I wondered, did that world bring him into contact with the lice-covered, emaciated little children he now agonized over?

"With the elections just over," he continued, "it is . . . it is . . . how would you say it? 'A whole new ball game.' Yes? We are dealing with new people. We are starting all over again. I am very much afraid that if you continue to try to go through the official channels, you will wait . . . perhaps another four years . . . perhaps forever. . . ."

"So what do we *do*?" I asked him.

"There are ways, Señora. There are always ways. But unfortunately they are expensive. . . ."

"How expensive?"

The lawyer looked a bit taken aback. He evidently had not expected me to get quite so directly to the heart of the matter. I watched him scribbling some figures, and I guessed he was trying to figure out what I was good for. There was a long silence, and when finally he looked up I saw that I was right.

"Because it is for the children," he said, "I will charge only four hundred dollars. Two hundred U.S. dollars paid now to cover my expenses. Then two hundred more when I deliver the papers. . ."

"*Four hundred dollars* just to get one signature!"

"Señora," he said, smiling thinly, "I am not unaware that there are substantial profits to be made in the business you are in. I have been told what American families are willing to pay for a child. . ."

I started to protest. Scotty cut me off. "Will you give us a few minutes," he asked the lawyer, "to discuss the terms of your offer?"

"Of course." The man rose politely from his desk. "May I have coffee sent in, Señora, while you talk?"

I was so angry I almost asked if he charged for that too. But Scotty's look said shut up. The lawyer left the room, closing the door unctuously behind him.

"No way!" I exploded as soon as we were alone. "I won't pay a dime to that snake. I mean, we're down here trying to help his country's kids, and he's trying to squeeze us for four hundred bucks? Come on!"

"Listen, Barbara," said Scotty, "four hundred dollars isn't going to kill us, and if this guy comes through we're going to have access to a real mother lode of kids who can be adopted with half the paperwork we're having to do now."

"It's my money, Scotty."

"It's only two hundred dollars of your money lost if he doesn't come through. I think it's a gamble worth taking."

I had to agree. The lawyer came back in. I pulled out my traveler's checks. He protested. "These matters are so awkward, Señora, but I must insist on cash. Your traveler's checks are only redeemable in our own currency. And dollars, as you know, can go a great deal further than quetzales in this unhappy economy of ours. You understand, of course?"

I understood that the man was probably making himself an easy two hundred U.S. dollars, but I paid him cash.

We left that afternoon for the village of San Félix. San Félix was the home of Juanita, without whose friendship we would never have won the trust of the impoverished local population. Scotty had met Juanita many years before when he was a member of the Franciscan Order stationed in Honduras and she was a girl of 20 just returned from the United States, where she had been sent by a wealthy expatriate American woman to study Baldwin School teaching techniques.

Juanita eventually started her own school, and Scotty had stayed in touch with her during his years as a priest in Central America. He had helped her lobby for sewer and water facilities for the town, helped her find funding to bring the local Indian children into her school, and watched as she became in the eyes of the people the unofficial "mayor" of San Félix. So we turned to Juanita for help when we began our adoption agency.

She had not disappointed us. Juanita's support gave us credibility and enabled the people in the area to trust us. She knew how to console a desperate mother who had decided that adoption was her child's best hope for a decent future, she could lead that mother through the surrender process in the local court, and she could keep the papers moving. I had no illusions about where we would have been if it had not been for the friendship of this remarkable, vivacious, dark-eyed woman.

I tried to relax. José was driving, Scotty was beside him talking a blue streak, and I had the back seat to myself. But relaxing wasn't easy on these narrow mountain roads lined with neat little white crosses marking the spots where some earlier motorists had gone off the edge. We wound our way down the side of one mountain range and crossed a low flat valley we called "the desert" because of its stifling midday heat. Then up into the mountains again and finally, near dusk, we saw in the valley below San Félix aglow in the light of the setting sun. José stopped the car. From this vantage point we couldn't see the barrios that hung precariously on the sides of the surrounding hills, or smell the open sewers that ran into the river. We saw only brightly painted houses nestled between two churches and smelled only the vines and flowers beside the road.

I caught my breath at the beauty of the scene. I looked down at the closer of the two cathedrals, with its huge, two-story-high wooden doors, its elaborate gardens, and its ornate iron fence. My eyes traveled across the Indian marketplace and across the rows of humble houses to the second church, this one built in the style of Byzantium. Two monuments, I thought sadly, to the forces committed to maintaining the status quo in Guatemalan society. Then José started the car again, and we went down past tiny farms clinging to the side of the mountain into the village.

Juanita was expecting us, a petite, brown-eyed bundle of energy, looking a bit older and more tired than when last we'd met but still with the same wonderful smile. The usual round of *abrazos* commenced, and then we moved on to a dinner that began cheerfully enough and then turned, too suddenly for this part of the world, to business. Juanita spoke of her increasing difficulty in finding kids. Adoptions, particularly adoptions by Americans, were becoming a controversial issue in Guatemalan society. The Church had always been opposed. Now politicians, riding the bandwagon of growing anti-Americanism, were inflaming crowds with talk of selling Guatemalan children to the gringos. Her own position as a liberated woman in a traditional society made her suspect.

"So what do we do?" I asked.

Juanita didn't know. There was one hope, a faint one. A social worker new in town, a woman named Alicia, had come from San Mateo in the north and reported seeing there a hospital filled with Indian children injured, or orphaned, or both, in the bitter civil war raging in that part of the country. There might be some chance the authorities might release two children for adoption.

"It's a government hospital?" I asked.

"It is," she said. "Evidently a blockhouse surrounded by barbed wire and guarded by soldiers. The government is under siege in San Mateo."

Scotty read my thoughts. "Barbed wire or not, we can't get in there" he declared. "Not until we get that damned piece of paper the lawyer has promised us."

"Maybe they'd let us in if we told them our papers were on the way," I suggested.

"Maybe we won't need the papers," said Juanita. "The government's pretty weak up there now. Maybe permission from the doctor in charge of the hospital would be enough to get the children out."

"Then let's go up there and find out," said Scotty. "Tonight!"

"Tonight?" I asked.

"Sure. Tonight. Every day we wait, the situation in the north will just get more precarious. Besides," he added with a grin, "blond-haired gringo ladies attract less attention when they move at night!"

"He's right," agreed Juanita. "My social-worker friend has given me the name of the hospital's head nurse, who might be able to get us in. There'll be fewer people on the night shift, so *all* of us will attract less attention."

"How long a drive is it?" I asked.

"Four hours," said José, "if we don't get stopped by a patrol."

So we went. José and Scotty took turns driving. Juanita and I slept as best we could in the back seat of our tiny Volkswagen. I was vaguely aware that the country we were crossing was getting higher. We drove through a mountain village that, with its moonlit church steeple and well-used white cottages nestled into the hills, reminded me of Switzerland. As the moon set behind the mountains, we reached the first military checkpoint. Soldiers looking not much older than children surrounded the car, curious about the *mujer americana* in the back seat. José did the talking. I was able to follow his rapid-fire Spanish well enough to understand that he was describing me as a nurse. Nurses were less controversial than women suspected of buying up children for the gringos.

The soldier in charge of the detail saluted. José ground into first gear, and we were off again into the now pitch-black night. Two checkpoints later we arrived in San Mateo. José pulled up in front of a cantina lit by a single lightbulb hanging from the ceiling. Scotty went inside and came back out with directions to the home of the head nurse. "Four houses down on the left," he grinned, as he climbed back into the car. I could tell that he was excited. My partner thrived on risks. I didn't.

Lights still burned in the head nurse's small stucco house. Juanita knocked on the door. A heavy-set woman answered. I could see children behind her, peeking around her skirts. The woman and Juanita talked briefly. Then the woman disappeared for a moment and came back out wearing a shawl. She and Juanita squeezed in beside me. "I do this," she said, "because you are friends of Alicia."

We drove in silence to the hospital. Barbed wire surrounded the building, and a thick-walled bunker stood behind the closed gate. The nurse showed her pass through the wire to a guard, who inspected it by flashlight before opening the gate. José drove through. I climbed stiffly out of the back and heard the guard's surprised exclamation as his light caught my blond hair.

We followed the nurse silently through the hospital lobby and down long empty halls to the nurse's station, where they found the *enfermera* in charge of the night shift. The nurse introduced us. I heard myself being described as an American who wanted to help children. Most of the rest I missed. But I had the impression that the *enfermera* saw our midnight arrival as a problem she could have done without.

She led us down the hall to the children's ward. I followed her between two rows of white cribs and saw in each one an emaciated little brown figure staring back at me. Some with open sores. Some with casts. Some with horribly distended bellies. "Oh no!" I said, near tears.

"*Sí,*" said the night nurse, speaking slowly so that I could understand. "They are all from the same village, Señora. The rebels came in and killed everybody. These are the children they didn't find or else left for dead."

I wondered why Indian rebels would have killed Indian children. I wondered if the murderers hadn't really been government soldiers retaliating against a village that supported the rebels. But I kept these thoughts to myself. "All orphans?" I asked.

"Not all. A few have mothers or fathers who were not in the village on the night the rebels came."

"Can I pick them up? Those without injuries?"

"Of course, Señora. But be careful. Some have soiled themselves. I am alone here at night, and I cannot keep up."

I counted the cribs. Twenty of them arranged in two rows of ten, each one with a numbered card at its foot. I started down one row, moving slowly from crib to crib. The children I picked up and tried to cuddle looked up at me, dull eyed and unresponsive.

Scotty passed me going the other way. "Take a look at the darling little girl in number seven," I whispered as we met. "She'd be perfect for the Partridges."

"You might not want to look in 19," he whispered back. "Poor little guy's not going to make it."

Of course I *did* look in number 19. I put my hand on a little head that felt like a hot cannonball and with my handkerchief wiped away the drool and sweat that crusted around the child's mouth. His head hung limp as I picked him up. I cradled him in my arms and felt him stir. Brown eyes looked up into mine. I smiled and then suddenly the child smiled back at me. I put him gently back in his crib. Scotty was wrong. If I could get him out, this child would make it! I *would* get him out. He *would* make it. He *had* to make it.

"Number 19 is going to the Warberg-Joneses," I told Scotty when we met at the end of the ward. He looked at me oddly.

The night nurse was getting uneasy. "It is time you left here, Señora," she urged. "It is against regulations. The doctor in charge will not be happy when she learns that I have let you visit the children."

"We'll talk to the doctor tonight," said Juanita. "I'm sure she'll approve entirely of your help to us."

The guard passed us out through the gate. "Do you really think we should bother the doctor tonight?" I asked Juanita. "It's already one o'clock."

"Better we bother her tonight than that she learn tomorrow that we've been inside his hospital without her permission," she said. "Besides, Barbara, here in the land of the siesta, one o'clock isn't an unheard-of hour for a visit."

We dropped the nurse off at her house and went on to the doctor's. Her house was identical—a simple structure of stuccoed cinder block. The lights were on. Juanita again went to the door and again a woman answered, this one an Indian with downcast eyes. "*La doctora no está en casa,*" I heard her say.

"*Cuando vuelve a la casa?*" asked Juanita.

"*Yo no se, señora. Está visitando un paciente.*"

"*Podemos esperar.*"

"*Bueno, señora.*" The woman did not invite us inside. We sat in the car, waiting, and 20 minutes later another car with only one headlight pulled up behind ours. We all got out to meet the doctor. Juanita introduced us and explained our mission. The woman was plainly exhausted but saw no choice but to ask us in. So we all trooped into her office and arranged ourselves on folding metal chairs in front of her battered mahogany desk. The doctor sat down, rubbed her eyes, squared her sagging shoulders, and asked me the question I always dreaded. "You have authorization from the ministry, Señora?"

"We've been assured that our agency's approval is imminent," I told her. "Until now we've been arranging private adoptions, mostly of Indian children from San Félix. I have photographs of some of these children and their new families if you would care to see them."

The doctor nodded wearily, and I launched into what Scotty called my "dog and pony show." I showed her pictures of little girls in pretty dresses posing with proud, fair-haired parents; of bright-eyed babies embracing sleek-coated dogs; of family picnics, of kindergarten classes, of nice boats and nice houses and nice cars, all filled with smiling people displaying their smiling little Indian children.

The doctor looked up from the album. "The Americans in your pictures have clothes and cars and boats, and then one day they decide they want a child," she said. "So they buy one. Yes?"

I pointed to a picture of the Partridges. "These two are hard-working farmers. Not rich at all. Yet for their entire married life they've been spending every cent they can scrape together on fertility clinics and special diets and God knows what else, all in the desperate hope of being able to conceive a child. Surely you agree that little Yolanda in crib number seven would be better off in their care than if. . . ."

She finished the sentence for me. "Better off than if she stayed here to be raised in poverty."

"Yes. If you want to put it that way, yes."

And she probably wanted to add but didn't, "and if she survives, she grows up to spawn more miserable, parasite-ridden children such as herself? Is it fair to pick only a few?"

"Would you deprive one child of happiness for the sake of some abstract commitment to fairness?" demanded Scotty. "God knows, we'd take every child in that ward of yours with us if we could! But life isn't fair. So let us at least do the little good we can do."

"I have heard stories," said the doctor. "Stories that our children are imported to the United States to be used as donors for organ transplants and then discarded like empty boxes."

"You actually believe that?" I gasped.

She held up her hand. "Señora, I am not saying that you do these things. I am saying only that I hear rumors that they are done. I have heard of adoption agencies that sell our children as commodities to the highest bidder, and of others that sell the *promise* of children to gullible families such as your Partridges and deliver only pictures."

"I can put you in touch with the families for whom we have found children. I'll give you their phone numbers," I told him. "I'll even pay for the calls. You can ask them if we do these things."

"I don't know if I can trust you Americans. I don't know if it's even possible to get these children released to you. Perhaps they are, after all, better off to stay here for many reasons."

I found myself on my feet, leaning over the doctor's desk, red faced and furious. "Forgive me also, Doctor. I'm tired too, but are you telling me there is redemption in misery? Purity in squalor? That's hogwash, Doctor, and you know it! Do you think that that mother who just died while you were delivering her child would not have exchanged the purity of her condition for a chance to live? Do you think she wouldn't have seized the chance we offer for a better life for her child? How can you let these children stay here to die in these cribs? I don't believe, as you seem to, that suffering should be extolled as a virtue!"

Scotty pushed me back into my seat. "*Señora doctora,*" he said quietly, "I know that you have good reason to suspect our motives. I've heard the same stories as you. There *are* crooked adoption agencies. I can only ask you to believe that ours isn't one of them. I beg you to let us have the children! For their sake and for the sake of two decent couples who will give them the love and care they need, let us take them with us."

"Señor McTaggart," said the doctor not unkindly, "even if I was persuaded that allowing you to take away those two children was the right thing to do, I could not do it. You see, my hospital's survival, and perhaps mine as well, depends on our remaining out of the public eye. If you took those two babies, there would be questions. Photographs, perhaps, in the press."

"Would you sacrifice those children just to spare your government some embarrassment?" I asked him. "What about the little boy in 19! I blurted. "He will surely die. Doesn't anyone care?"

"If he dies, it is God's will. And now, Señora, if you will excuse me? As I said, I am very tired."

We drove back through the fading night to San Félix. "We'll call the lawyer," I said desperately. "We'll tell him a child's life depends on getting those papers to us immediately."

José, who had said little all during that long night, answered me. "You could be risking 18 lives to save 2," he said quietly. "So you see, Barbara, the equation is not a good one."

*   *   *

Scotty and I flew back to Miami three days later. Scotty broke tradition and sat beside me on the flight home. Kind soul that he is, he sensed my despair.

"I don't know if I can do this any longer," I told him as our plane circled for altitude above the road we had so recently traveled. "Seeing all those kids. . . knowing they're going to die and not being able to do a thing to help them. . . it's tearing me up, Scotty. It really is."

"I don't think we *can* do it any longer, Barbara," he said quietly. "If our currency is kids, then the firm is bankrupt. Our sources have dried up."

"José knew all along, didn't he?"

"I think he did."

"So why did he put us onto that slick lawyer?"

"It has to do with hope, Barbara. What you are seeing is a kind of Central American double-think. As long as nothing gets done, then everything remains possible. It's why papers and rubber stamps and notaries and *funcionarios* and perhaps even priests figure so prominently in life down here."

"It's a strange world, isn't it?"

"It's an unfair world!"

"So it would seem. I mean, look at us. We played by the rules. We assumed, at least I assumed, that because most people are basically decent, then if you try to do a good thing, it'll happen. But it didn't. I wonder why? I mean, when you've got parents that need kids and kids that need parents, it just shouldn't be that hard to get them together."

"It shouldn't be. But it is."

2

Documents resplendent with stamps and ribbons

*I*N 1980 David and I were living on Cape Cod with our two biological children, Chris, 12, and Karen, 10. My husband and I had
grown up together, first setting eyes on each other when we were
young children and he was living with his mother and grandparents in
Wareham after his father had been killed piloting a bomber over
Germany. My family frequently visited relatives who lived next to
David's grandparents, and these various grown-ups tried valiantly to
get us to play together. I was game but David always took off like a shot
whenever I was in the area, so I didn't see much of him but the dust he
left behind.

My own father's family came from Germany and my mother's from
Cape Cod. They met when she was 18, married a year later, and spent
the next six years alternately working or cruising, depending on the
state of their finances. World War II interrupted this idyll. Dad joined
the Navy and Mom returned to Centerville on the Cape, where I spent
the first years of my life. We moved to Winchester after the war, and
Dad set up an automobile dealership that provided an income while he
indulged his real passion, which was inventing gadgets in his workshop
behind the house.

He'd once flown biplanes, which somehow led him to invent some kind of widget that is now widely used in the manufacture of jet airplane engines. I'm not sure what Dad's widget does, but I do know that it made him a lot of money and that today it allows David and me the financial independence to live our lives without worrying about where our next meal is coming from. Dad died in a tragic drowning accident in 1981, just as this story was beginning to unfold.

David and I were brought together, after his years of escape and evasion, by an antique truck he had rebuilt. Pride in his truck overrode his shyness, and he offered me a ride. Off we went, winding our way on old dirt roads through the Wareham woods, and the ice was broken. Not long after that eventful ride, David joined the Coast Guard and I went off to college. We saw what we could of each other during the next four years and married as soon as he got out. I was 21. We bought a rundown old Cape Cod house and fixed it up. David worked in a boat yard and I finished college. I began work part-time as a social worker in our local hospital. A year or so later I became a social worker with the Massachusetts Department of Public Welfare. Our son, Chris, was born the next year and our daughter, Karen, two years after that.

And so the pattern of our lives was established. Thirteen happy years went by. We decided to stop at two children, a decision dictated by both our commitment to the idea of zero population growth and the fact that we lived in a small house. But then, one January afternoon in 1980, all that changed.

I was in the kitchen when I heard David's truck come up the drive. I listened to the familiar sound of footsteps crunching across gravel as he walked over to the barn to put away his tools and was waiting for him when he came in the back door. "Good day?" I asked.

"The usual," he grinned. "How about yours?"

"Horrible!" I said. "I spent the afternoon with that McCoy girl over in Brewster. She's just had another baby. Her fifth, and she's got no idea who the father is. Same as with the last one."

David's mind was off somewhere else. "Oh?" he said through a mouth full of Oreo cookies. "Too bad. . ."

"It is too bad!" I said, suddenly upset. "Poor kid hasn't even got a name! Can you believe that? I mean, what kind of life is a kid going to have when his mother doesn't even care enough to give him a name?"

"Any chance she'd put him up for adoption?"

"Don't think I haven't tried to persuade her! 'No way,' she says. 'Ain't nobody gonna take my kid away from me!' The usual line."

"Can't the courts do something?"

"Not likely. 'Keep families together!' That's our policy. Costs the tax-payer less!"

"Cynic!"

"Damn right I am! It's driving me nuts, David! I see so many of these poor kids, and I feel so powerless to help them! God! I'd like to adopt them all!"

David grinned. "One maybe. That I could go along with. But not all of them!"

*   *   *

Our decision to adopt did not come entirely out of the blue. Talking with David about all the human tragedies my work put me in contact with over the years had become something of a safety valve for me. I'd come home night after night heartbroken about some poor child and pour out the whole sad story to my long-suffering husband. He'd listen patiently, and invariably these tales of mine about families that had so little of love and security would remind us of our own good fortune at having such an abundance of both. Our own children were now teenagers and increasingly striking off on lives of their own. We'd had such fun with our two rambunctious hellions that the idea of bringing another child in under our happy tent, coupled with the almost daily reminder that there were so many needy kids out there, made the idea of adoption evolve naturally for both of us.

So it was decided. I made an appointment with the adoption people in my department, and the following week David and I drove up to Boston to a ramshackle public building on Washington Street, where I found myself in the unfamiliar position of being interviewed by one of my own colleagues.

My social worker was a young man, still a bit nervous with strangers. He told us that having two children of our own basically disqualified us from adopting an unimpaired infant. But we did qualify for a handicapped child of any age or for an unimpaired child of six years or older.

David was uneasy about taking on an older child. I replied that there were advantages to getting a child who arrived already toilet trained.

That clinched the argument. We agreed on taking an older child.

That same day we were assigned to a class with other prospective parents and shown a movie about the children in the custody of the state. The film pulled no punches. Our classmates laughed nervously at the bizarre antics of some disturbed children and gasped at the sight of others with horribly disfiguring handicaps. I had seen it all before.

"Poor little buggers," David said as we left the building. "You sure you want to go ahead with this?"

I said I was.

"Funny," he said, taking my hand. "I'm more sure now than I was before I saw that film."

We went home and started the endless job of filling out forms. Then we waited. In May, our social worker called to say that the rules had changed and that Department of Public Welfare social workers were no longer eligible to apply for public adoptions. The rationale for this change of policy was that since caseworkers were sometimes required to testify in court against incompetent parents, conflicts of interest were possible if we could apply to adopt children the department might have taken away from their natural families.

"So what do we do now?" I asked him.

"You could quit your job," he said. "Either that or apply to a private adoption agency."

David and I made another trip to Boston, this time to the Protestant Social Services Center, where we were shown another movie, given a new set of forms to fill out, and then, after another long wait, again declared ineligible because of my association with the Department of Public Welfare.

"Christ!" said David, "let's just make a kid of our own. Be one hell of a lot easier!"

"For you, maybe!" I tried to laugh but it didn't come out right.

David put his arm around me. "This is starting to get to you, isn't it, Barb?"

"It is," I said. "It hurts every time we get our hopes up and then get turned down."

"So what do you say we just sit on this a while?" he suggested. "Let's let the summer go by, and if we still want to adopt a kid in September we'll start again. Okay?"

I agreed to that. It was a strange time for both of us. I don't think our commitment to adopt a child was any less. But we both found ourselves having to deal with unexpected emotions. When you make up your mind to bring a new baby into your family and you work long and hard to make that happen and find yourself blocked at every turn, the experience is, I imagine, not dissimilar to the hell infertile couples must go through. We were just worn out. We needed time to muster the emotional energy to get back into the fight.

*   *   *

We regained our energy by September. We'd hashed out a lot of things between us during the months we'd been on hold. David was still uneasy about the genetic baggage a child of unknown parents might come carrying. I was more of the opinion that every child began as a blank slate. I agreed with my husband that heredity might have some bearing on the size of that slate, but I argued that the child's parents did most of the writing on it. I conceded that genes might determine if a child grew up to be an Einstein or an auto mechanic. But I believed, as I still do, that although genes have something to do with whether a child grows up to be a decent and compassionate human being, those qualities come mostly from the parents.

"So how do you explain good parents who end up with bad kids?" David asked. "It happens. You know it does."

"Of course I do. I know that the child we adopt might have problems. But doesn't even a kid with problems stand a better chance in a decent family than in no family at all? Won't it be enough if we just make things better for this child than they would have been otherwise?"

David agreed.

So I telephoned an organization called the Open Door Society. The Open Door Society served as sort of an unofficial information center for agencies that arrange international adoptions, and there I reached the first person I found in the adoption business who seemed more interested in getting around obstacles than in creating them. Her name was Betty Laning, and she suggested I get in touch with a Quincy-based agency named Making Family Connections, which had contacts in El Salvador. But, she warned, she could make no guarantees. All she really knew was that she'd heard nothing bad about Making Family Connections, and that was a lot more than she could say for some of the agencies that worked abroad. International adoption, said Betty Laning, was a very minimally regulated industry.

We decided to risk it. Making Family Connections sent us an information packet that included instructions for the procedures to be followed in an international adoption, a contract, and a fee schedule that called for $300 up front, a $3,500 "out of country fee" for the lawyer in El Salvador, and an additional $300 payable on delivery.

The first step outlined in the procedures was that David and I undergo a state-mandated home study by a licensed social worker. I was surprised but not unhappy about this requirement, because it meant that there was at least some public oversight of international adoptions. I was familiar with home studies from my own work and was glad to see them also required for families adopting from overseas.

David was less enthusiastic about opening up our family to some stranger. "You're a licensed social worker," he suggested. "Why don't you write a letter declaring us a model couple? Throw in a picture of the dog and a xerox of your last bill from Jordan Marsh. They'll love us!"

"Birdsey inspects Birdsey! I don't think it'll fly."

The social worker turned out to be someone from my own regional office who moonlighted for Making Family Connections. Her name was Judy, and it took her three long visits with us to get through the home study check list. She asked us how we had gotten along with our own parents. We told her fine. She asked us how we'd dealt with the problem of infertility. We pointed to Chris and Karen. She asked David if he or anyone in his family would object to a dark-skinned male child carrying the family name. He said not so far as he knew. She measured our house, divided the total square footage by the number of occupants plus one, and concluded that we had room enough for another child. She examined our bank statements and declared us solvent. And finally she raised certain delicate subjects she lumped together under the heading "Sticky Issues." Had there been previous marriages? Arrests? Natural children from our own union or other unions in our pasts whom we had surrendered for adoption? We said no.

"Well then," said Judy, "I guess you pass!"

"You haven't asked us if we are now or ever have been members of the Communist Party," said David with a grin.

"That question's not on the list," she said. "I'll bring it to the attention of my superiors!"

*   *   *

Next we began the task of assembling the documents necessary to support our applications to the U.S. Immigration and Naturalization Service for a form I600A ("Preliminary Approval to Adopt a Foreign National") and to the Salvadorean government for permission to export a child.

We needed: Birth certificates (copies not acceptable; actual signatures from the town clerk required). David's document, from his home town in Texas, took three weeks and what seemed like three hundred phone calls to acquire.

Fingerprints. We went down to the Barnstable Police Station and were printed by a surly desk sergeant who seemed to be trying to break my fingers in the process.

A letter from the police chief testifying that we were good citizens. I went again to the police station.

"Sorry, Ma'am," said the chief. "I can't write that."

"Why not? We've never been arrested for anything."

"I'll have to check into it, Ma'am. I've never done this kinda thing before. I'm just not comfortable with the procedure."

Rather than wait for him to get comfortable with the procedure, I drove up and got a letter from the Office of Probation in Boston declaring David and myself free of criminal records.

We also needed complete physical examinations, including physician's assessment of subjects' capacity to parent; statements of assets and liabilities; marriage certificate (copy not acceptable); IRS form 1040 for the past two years; birth certificates for existing children; deeds for all real estate owned; letters of recommendation (three); letters from our employers certifying that we were not about to be laid off; and, finally, psychological evaluations to include the psychiatrist's or psychologist's assessment of our capacity to parent.

Everything had to be notarized. It took us five months to do it, but finally we had it all together.

Our contact at Making Family Connections was a woman named Sandra Bush, whom I never met personally but to whom I spoke often enough on the phone to decide she wasn't the sharpest pencil in the pack. But for us she *was* Making Family Connections, so I called her yet again to ask what next.

She told us we were to take our packet up to the secretary of state's office on the seventh floor of the McCormick Building in Boston and have them certify our papers for adoption. "But," said Sandra, "you'd better hurry. Your FD280 fingerprint forms are only good for twelve months and you've already used up five of them. If your FD280 expires, you've got to start all over again."

We rushed up to the McCormick Building and presented ourselves to the secretary of state's office. "How many papers to be certified?" asked the clerk.

"Twenty-one in all," I said.

"Cost you three dollars per document. Come back in three hours and we'll have 'em done for you."

"What is it exactly that you do?"

"We authenticate the notaries. Check that their commissions haven't expired."

I pushed David out the door before he exploded. We came back in three hours. "Got 'em all done for you," said the clerk. "All except your assets and liabilities statement. That one wasn't notarized."

"But it's the original! My husband compiled that one himself."

"Sorry. We've got no way of knowing that. You'll have to come back."

We gathered up our 21 papers, 20 of them now adorned with a new cover page bearing the Great Seal of the Commonwealth, paid $60, and drove home. When we got there, I found a letter from the Immigration and Naturalization Service. "Dear Sir/Madam," said the letter. "Your form FD280 is being returned as unacceptable for the reason stated below." There was a big red "X" in the box next to "Prints Smeared" and another note to the effect that our I600A application could not be processed until our form FD280 was resubmitted.

So we went back to the police station and back to the McCormick building and back to Making Family Connections, and, finally, 11 months after we had begun assembling the evidence of our acceptability, we were at last able to mail everything off to the Salvadorean consulate in New York City. There, for an additional five dollars per document, each one of our papers received another cover page, this one bearing a handsome ribbon showing the colors of the country from whence someday might come our child.

*   *   *

We felt as if, after a long quest, we had finally found the Holy Grail. Those documents, resplendent with stamps and ribbons, had by now taken on an almost mystical quality for us. Those documents *were* our child. We handled them with reverence, stacked them carefully with edges exactly aligned, checked and rechecked that everything was in order, and when we were finally convinced that it was, we sent them off special delivery in December of 1981 to Making Family Connections with a request for female child, two years old or younger.

We found ourselves oddly grateful for the long bureaucratic ordeal. We'd been through the fire. Our resolve had been tested, not once but many times, and we had carried on. We had proven to ourselves that our decision to take on another son or daughter was not just some romantic dream rooted in nostalgic memories of the time when our own marriage and our own two children were still young. We had *earned* our next child.

We did not know that our ordeal was far from over.

Sandra Bush explained to us what was supposed to happen. Our papers would be sent to the lawyer who represented Making Family Connections in El Salvador. He in turn would get in touch with his contacts in orphanages and maternity hospitals, locate a prospective child, and mail us a photograph and biographical information. Once we approved his choice, he would begin court proceedings to arrange the adoption. And when that was done, all we would have to do was fly to El Salvador and pick up our child.

"How long will it take?" David and I asked together.

Sandra Bush said it wouldn't be long.

Spring came and with it no word from Making Family Connections. I called them up and was told that there had been a delay in mailing the papers. Our application had had to wait for two other couples to complete theirs so all three could be processed at once. But we were not to worry. The papers were now on their way to El Salvador, and everything was on track.

I did worry. Why hadn't Making Family Connections at least told us there would be a delay? "Because we're very busy," said Sandra Bush.

We still hadn't heard anything by August. I called a friend of mine in the State Department to ask his advice. He wasn't optimistic. "If your papers have already been in country three months and you haven't heard anything," my friend cautioned, "then the odds are you're not going to. My bet is that your agency's source of kids has dried up."

I again called Sandra Bush and told her bluntly that if her agency could not deliver, we were going to look for someone who could. "If that's what you want to do," she said, not trying to hide the irritation in her voice, "but remember that a lot of international adoption agencies are going out of business because they can't find kids. I can tell you that all our clients who have been willing to wait have received a child. You'll just have to be as patient as everyone else."

I hung up. Sandra Bush was another of the many people I'd met since we'd begun this odyssey who somehow managed to make me feel guilty. Everyone from police chiefs to clerks all seemed to react to me as if I was trying to do something illegal or immoral. I was getting kind of sick of it. "It's the squeaky wheel that gets the grease," I told David. "Maybe it's time we started to squeak."

From that point on I called Making Family Connections once a month, and each time Sandra Bush told me to be patient. Finally in March of 1983 our patience ran out and we began contacting other agencies. One, in Atlanta, Georgia, sounded promising but warned us we would have to wait a minimum of another 18 months if they took over our case. I asked them to send us an application.

In late March, Sandra Bush notified us that Making Family Connections had found us a four-year-old girl. I reminded her that we'd asked for a child two years old or younger.

"We know that," she said, "but the judge in El Salvador feels that you're both too old for a child of that age. This is your chance, Mrs. Birdsey. I wouldn't let it go by."

"But how did our papers even get before a judge?" I asked her. "I thought we had to approve the child before adoption proceedings began?"

"Mrs. Birdsey," said Sandra Bush, "you *have* to trust us. Adoptable children are scarce and getting scarcer. If you don't want this child, there are a lot of other couples who do. You're going to have to make up your mind. I'll need an answer tonight."

"*Tonight?*" I felt myself on the edge of panic. "We don't even have a picture! We don't know anything about this girl. . . "

"I'm sorry," she said, "but that's the way it is in this business. We've got to move fast or we'll lose the child."

I gathered our family for an emergency session to discuss this prospective new daughter. Chris and Karen were noncommittal. Their enthusiasm at the prospect of a little sister had faded in the nearly two years since we had first suggested the idea, and now the best I could get out of them was, "Whatever you and Dad want to do, Mom. It's okay with us."

David and I agonized far into the night. He was for insisting on more information even at the risk of losing the child. I wasn't sure I dared wait. Maybe in El Salvador children just went to the highest bidder? Maybe some other agency was competing for this same child? Maybe Making Family Connections's option was about to run out? I bombarded David with maybes.

"Maybe that's also why they're telling us so little about this child," he said. "This whole damn thing feels too much like buying a car. 'You gotta act fast!'" he mimicked. "'They won't last long at these rock-bottom prices, and supplies are limited!'"

"Supplies are limited, David! This may be our only chance."

So finally we agreed to take the child.

More papers arrived special delivery from Making Family Connections. We filled them out, returned them also by special delivery, and waited. Three weeks later the phone rang late at night. A woman named Paula Brown was on the line; she introduced herself as an adoptive parent who'd worked with Making Family Connections and had just returned from El Salvador.

"Off the record," she warned, "the little girl you've spoken for is at least six years old. Maybe older. The reason they've been able to present her as younger is because she's horribly undernourished. There's a good chance she's brain damaged."

I thanked her, put down the phone numbly, and tried to tell David what I'd just heard. But it was a long time before I could get the words out.

The next morning I called Making Family Connections and lost my temper. Sandra Bush was for once subdued, and I sensed she was genuinely upset that the child she had found for us had been so sadly misrepresented by her agency's contacts in El Salvador. The only advice she had left to offer was that we withdraw our current application and apply again to Guatemala, where Making Family Connections had recently been having better luck. She explained that her agency worked in Guatemala through an intermediary named Sue Hampson, who was the proprietor and single employee of an outfit called Adopting Oveseas. Sue Hampson had no license, which is why she relied on Making Family Connections to do her paperwork.

It all sounded pretty shaky. But we were in this fight now, and we weren't going to quit. Our friends asked us why we kept beating our heads against the wall. Didn't we already have two fine children of our own? Wasn't that enough? God knows, we asked ourselves those same questions many, many times. I don't think either one of us could put our answer into words. But I imagine anyone who has tried to have another child and couldn't would understand.

* * *

When I met Sue Hampson, I thought I had run into a whirlwind. I'd made the two hour drive to New London, Connecticut, found a split-level house with the right number on it, and walked up to the door, not knowing quite what to expect. A pretty brunette woman of about my age, dressed in a housecoat and surrounded by children of all shapes and sizes, answered my knock. "This is my kennel," she hollered above the sound of many voices speaking Spanish, English, and everything in between. "Come in if you dare!"

I inched my way into the house, with Sue running interference ahead of me. "Ricardo! Bobby! Cita!" she yelled cheerfully, *"Vayase! Vayase, niños!"* Grinning blue- and brown-eyed urchins scuttled in all directions as we pushed our way into the kitchen. "Corporate Headquarters!" grinned Sue, indicating the kitchen table.

"Are these all *yours*?" I asked, waving at the pack of kids who now peered at me from behind the furniture.

"Far as I know!" said Sue. "They're all Hampsons if the paperwork's not screwed up, which it probably is. The paperwork's always screwed up! But I don't give a damn. I'll break every rule in the book if it'll get these little monkeys out of the hellholes they come from!" She grabbed a tiny boy from behind her chair and gave him a bearhug. "I'm crazy about my little munchkins!" she laughed. "Who wouldn't be?"

One of the two phones on the kitchen table rang. Sue picked it up, making a face at the interruption, and launched into a rapid-fire conversation in Spanish while I took a better look at this pleasant dervish, whom I liked already. I'd heard rumors that Sue's success in Central America was due at least in part to her having some well-placed friends in the governments she dealt with, and watching her now on the phone, I could believe it. When the lady across the table turned on the charm, the whole room lit up. I could follow only half the conversation, but I sensed that whoever was on the other end of that line was having one hell of a time saying no to whatever it was Sue wanted.

She finally hung up. "Jerk!" she said, scowling, and then, not missing a beat, turned her attention to me, talking in staccato bursts. "Sandra told me what happened. Too bad. Doesn't surprise me a bit. Lying bastards always misrepresent kids. Only way is go down and see for yourself. Whole goddamn system's a mess. . . ."

"You're telling me!" I said. And then suddenly I found myself pouring out all the unhappiness and frustrations of the past two years. "God, Sue, this has been the most awful experience we've ever been through. It's not the mountains of paperwork or the surly bureaucrats, those we can deal with. It's the waiting that's killing us. Waiting and waiting and waiting! And we don't even know who we're waiting for!"

"See it happening every day," said Sue. "And it's not only the prospective parents who get hammered. It's the kids, too. It breaks my heart seeing children shuttled around like goddamn commodities. But, believe me, that's all they are in some parts of the world!"

"Well," I said, "I guess talking about it won't change it. What can David and I do? What can *you* do?"

"What I can do," said Sue, "is get you a kid. But I've got to tell you, Barbara, I don't come cheap!" She gestured toward her plate-filled sink and mountains of unwashed laundry. "It takes money to maintain this lifestyle of the rich and famous! It'll cost you a thousand bucks for me to hook you up with a child, but I guarantee you'll get a good one! That a deal?"

"I guess it is," I said. "I guess I'm not going to find a better one."

*   *   *

David and I spent a frantic couple of weeks redoing our papers to conform to Guatemala's requirements and then delivered the package triumphantly to Sue Hampson. "These sat two years in El Salvador, Sue," we told her. "We're counting on you to move them a little faster in Guatemala!"

"Two years!" she said. "Sandra didn't tell me that! Christ, that changes everything! If your stuff's already been two years in El Salvador, somebody down there has already done something with them. Might be a hell of a lot faster if we build on what you got instead of starting off again cold in Guatemala. I got friends down there too."

Resubmitting to El Salvador meant another paper chase, but we did it. Sue's optimism was so infectious we didn't even begrudge her the wasted time and money spent processing our papers for Guatemala. Our package went off to El Salvador in September 1983 for a second time, and once again we settled down to wait.

In October, Sue called us to say she'd found us a 14-month-old girl in El Salvador. I was almost too excited to speak. "But that's. . . that's *great*, Sue!" I stammered into the phone. "What about your on-site inspection? We can fly down tonight if we need to."

"No need!" she said. "You can trust me on this one, Barbara. She's a darling little girl!"

I didn't even ask David. I said we'd take her.

The next month passed in a frenzy of buying baby stuff. Then, in January 1984, Sue called to say that our little girl had been claimed by relatives and was no longer available for adoption.

"Oh no!" I sobbed into the phone.

"Yeah," she said, "I know it's a bummer, Barb. But look, I got a month-old infant girl who's just been abandoned at Santa Teresa Hospital. I think we can get her."

"Do it!" I said. "We don't need pictures! We don't need anything! Just get that child! But please, Sue, *please* don't lose this one!" David and I had already decided that if we got a baby girl we were going to call her Tamsin, which was the family name of one of his great great-grandmothers. From the beginning we were happy with that decision, because she didn't look like a "Norma," which was her original name.

Sue said she would do her damnedest. A couple of days later she called again. "Not to worry!" she said right off. "Everything's still on track. I'm calling about something else. You're a licensed social worker, right?"

"Right."

"Good! That's just what I need. See, I've been trying to get legitimate. I've been filling out the papers to start my own agency, but you know how this kid is with papers! What I need is a partner who's legit. It would be one hell of a lot easier than going through Making Family Connections. Interested?"

Alarm bells started going off. I had a panicky thought that Sue might hold this new baby hostage to my saying yes. I tried to stall. I told her I'd have to think about it, talk to David, etc. But Sue the Whirlwind wasn't one to take no or even maybe for an answer.

"Tell you what," she interrupted. "I got three couples and three single parents waiting to pick up kids in El Salvador, but they're scared shitless because of the war. They want me to pick up their kids for them."

"Is that a problem?"

"Nope. Do it all the time. But how about you go? I'll get you the powers of attorney and your ticket. That way you get to see the business from both ends before you make up your mind. It would also give you the chance to see your own little girl. You won't be able to bring her home. Courts haven't approved your application yet. But you'll get to see her. How's that sound?"

It sounded better than sitting and waiting. I said I'd do it.

3

Ah jes' raise tomaters, Ma'am

TWO days later I found myself armed with some rather vague instructions from Sue and on the plane to El Salvador. I traveled with a friend of mine, Lucinda Smith, a ready-for-anything girl who came along because Salvadorean regulations required that one adult could travel with a maximum of two children. Lucinda's kids were friends with my kids, and we'd become good friends as well. She was an inspirational person, always calm, gentle, and loving, and she was sustained through more than her share of personal tragedy by an unwavering faith that everything, no matter how awful or apparently unfair, happened for a purpose that we would someday understand. This was her first trip to a Third World country, as it was for me, and the suffering we were to see there would test but not shake her faith in the existence of a Divine Plan.

On the plane we met Peter and Phyllis Lord, both lawyers, on their own mission to adopt a child. They were a remarkable couple, returning with open eyes for a second time after an earlier trip to El Salvador in search of a child had ended in failure. Ideally suited for the challenges of taking on an international adoption, they were well read, well traveled, and above all gutsy.

The airport where we landed in the afternoon of that mid-January day in 1984 was one and a half hours by taxi from downtown San Salvador. The four of us piled into a VW Beetle driven by a former university student who spoke English, and we set off through country that had suffered environmental destruction beyond anything I had ever seen before. For mile after mile we passed barren hills that had once been covered with upland jungle but were now stripped bare and horribly eroded. Fires still smoldered where farmers were burning off what little forest remained. "My God!" said Peter Lord. "They're burning their own futures!"

Our driver looked back at us in his mirror. "We have no future," he said simply.

We drove on in silence. As we neared the city, we began to see people huddled under cardboard shelters—first just a few families living in scattered settlements, then people by the thousands, packed into hillside slums. At one point we passed a soldier who seemed to be waving. We waved back and suddenly the road was filled with more soldiers, squinting at us down the barrels of automatic weapons. Our driver skidded to a stop and climbed out, ashen faced. I watched a cold-eyed sergeant slam the terrified boy up against the side of the car and go roughly through his documents. I heard his stammered explanation that no, he hadn't seen the roadblock, and yes, his passengers were just American tourists arriving from the airport. The sergeant looked curiously in the open car window, grinned at us with blackened teeth, and waved us on our way. "Christ!" said Peter, wiping the sweat from his face. "That's a first for me. I really thought for a minute they were actually going to start shooting!"

"They might have," said our still-shaken driver. "Government soldiers usually shoot first and find out who they've shot later."

Sue Hampson had booked us into a hotel halfway up the mountain, midway between the slums at the bottom and the high-walled houses of the very rich at the summit. After a long climb up narrow streets in second gear, we piled stiffly out of the Beetle and found ourselves in a setting reminiscent of southern California. A palm-lined walk ran past a swimming pool to the hotel entrance beyond. The only discordant note was that the place appeared to be abandoned.

We were standing uncertainly under a blue marquee when another taxi came laboring up the hill. As this ancient vehicle wheezed by us, its passenger, who looked for all the world like another destitute peasant, did a double take as his eyes caught mine. He said something to his driver; the taxi screeched to a halt and backed up to where we stood. The peasant jumped out and asked us in a thick New York accent what the goddamn hell we were doing standing alone on a street in San Salvador.

We were all four too dumbfounded to answer. "We're tourists," I said finally. Sue had warned me about being too open about our real mission. "American tourists. What's the matter with that?"

"What's the matter?" sputtered this apparition. "You'll get shot. That's what's the matter. But look, I gotta go. I'll be back around midnight, and I'll explain it all to you then. But don't even think about wandering around the city by yourselves, okay? That is unless you're CIA. If you're CIA, I don't give a damn what you do!"

The man climbed back into his taxi and was gone.

"CIA?" muttered Peter. "Guy's got to be some kind of nut case!"

I had to agree.

We found a clerk and checked in. Lucinda and I followed a silent porter down empty halls to our room, and, when he'd finally left us there after endless puttering around trying to run up his tip, we flopped down on our beds exhausted. "Don't you have the feeling you're dreaming all this, Barb?" my friend asked. "That none of it is really happening?"

I pushed aside the curtains and looked out the window. Our room was at the back of the hotel, facing downhill and overlooking the fetid slum below. "Palm trees and a pool out one window," said Lucinda, "slums and starving children out the other. What'd I tell you? We've *got* to be dreaming!"

There was a knock at our door. I opened it a crack without releasing the security chain and peeked out. A tiny woman stood in the hall, smiling uncertainly. "You have not to worry," she said in heavily accented English. "I am only Margarita. The lawyers who represent the children you have come for have asked me to be your escort."

So it was that we met the woman who in the days to come we

referred to fondly as our drill sergeant. Margarita was a tiny, grey-haired woman of French ancestry who did so much more to help us than her job required that we found ourselves depending on her almost entirely. I never learned how it was that she came to be in El Salvador. She spoke several languages and at one point had worked as an interpreter for a foreign company with a base in El Salvador, and that perhaps is what brought her to the attention of the attorneys Sue dealt with. She was patient and efficient, and she loved the people of her adopted country, especially the children. We grew to love her.

Margarita promptly took over. "The way it will be," she instructed, "is that the children will be brought here by the foster parents who have the custody. You have pictures. Yes?"

I nodded.

"Good!" said Margarita. "When the child is brought, you will look at your picture to make it sure you have the right one. Yes?"

"There's a chance I won't have the right one?" I asked.

"It is possible. Does the señora read Spanish?"

"Not well."

"Then I will handle the papers. All you must do is confirm that the child is the correct one. From the picture. Yes?"

"Yes."

"Then I will say goodbye until later, Señoras. My house is just down the street from the hotel entrance, so it will be convenient. You will only have to ask the front desk for Margarita, and they will send a boy for me. Yes?" With that she smiled her charming smile and left.

Day One of this surreal adventure unfolded just as Margarita said it would. The first taxi to arrive in front of our still empty hotel carried a sad, worn-out-looking woman and a little girl who followed silently behind her. The two of them were escorted up to our room, which we had hastily made over into a kind of receiving center.

I checked the file. This child, judging from her size, would be Julia, age seven, who was going to a single parent, a woman executive who lived in Boston. Lucinda confirmed the identification with the picture. Margarita sat on one bed, going through the papers the woman had brought with her. Julia went silently to a corner of the room. Trying to be cheerful, I gave her the doll her new mother had sent down for her. She took it without expression and continued to stand motionless with her new blond-haired, blue-eyed, pink-skinned doll dangling forlornly from one hand. Margarita completed her business. The tired woman seemed to be fighting back tears. She hugged little Julia fiercely and quickly left the room.

More children began arriving. I was soon so busy tending to tiny infants and trying to understand the instructions for their care from the women who brought them that I almost forgot about little Julia. But every time I looked up she was still there in her corner, holding her doll.

By mid-afternoon we had accepted custody of three infants, who lay howling in the bureau drawers we'd turned into impromptu cribs. All three of them had the diarrhea that Margarita told us was a nearly chronic condition in babies unaccustomed to milk. "What's their normal diet?" asked Phyllis over the din.

"Crushed fruit," said Margarita. "Their mothers can't afford milk."

Louder howling came from down the hall. Another foster parent arrived at the door towing a frantic three-year-old. "Carmelita?" I asked her, checking off the next to last name on my list.

"Sí, Señora," said the foster parent, and then she too burst into such a torrent of tears she seemed incapable of saying anything further. I looked helplessly at Margarita, who got up from the bed she'd been using as a desk and took the weeping woman in her arms. "It's hard for her," she explained as the woman's sobbing subsided. "You see, she has raised this child from birth."

I looked down and suddenly almost broke into tears myself. Julia had come out of her corner and was offering her doll to the little girl.

Peter and Phyllis Lord, meanwhile, were getting more and more nervous. The sun was already setting, and their own child had yet to arrive. Margarita advised patience. But the Lords were both take-charge types. They felt they ought to be *doing* something. Peter wanted to call his agency to find out if there'd been some mistake and find out whom they could talk to down here who had some *clout*. He paced back and forth and stepped over piles of diapers and around the drawers turned into cribs, while he pondered his options. All the while driving me nuts. I was about to scream at him *Just sit down for God's sake!* when the Lord's baby boy arrived. So I just watched, smiling to myself as this high-powered couple metamorphosed before my eyes into a cooing new Mom and Dad.

By then it was very late. The infants were asleep in their drawers. Julia and Carmelita, wide-eyed but silent, lay side-by-side in one of the beds with the doll between them. Margarita got up silently and tip-toed to the door. I followed her into the hall. The little woman smiled up at me. "Now," she said, "you begin to know what it is like. Yes?"

"I had no idea. . . ."

"I find it very sad that this country cannot care for its own children and so must send them away. But I know it is best for them. That is why I help. Yes?"

"I have two children of my own, Margarita. This day has made me wonder if I would have the courage to give them up. Even if I knew it was best for them, I don't know if I could do it."

"Then, Señora, I think I am glad that it is you who came to take them away. Tomorrow we and the children must go to the court. I will be here at eight o'clock, and you will have them dressed by that time. Yes?"

I went back to our room and convened a whispered council of war. The Lords wanted to spend a couple of hours alone with their new son, Jonathan, and then offered to spell Lucinda and me so we could go down to the hotel bar and get a drink. We checked our watches and found to our amazement that it was already ten o'clock. "Time flies when you're having fun!" grinned Lucinda. The Lords said they'd be back at 11:30 and went off to their own room.

It was nearly midnight by the time Lucinda and I finally got down to the bar. We both ordered gin and tonics. The bartender looked at us strangely, nodded, and came back with two glasses of coke. "Gosh," I groaned, "I didn't think my Spanish was *that* bad!

"*No Coca Cola, Señor,*" I said to the man. "*Yo quiero gin y tónica!*"

"*Sí, Señora, comprendo,*" he said and moved down to the other end of the bar.

"Maybe we should be flattered," laughed Lucinda. "Maybe he thinks we're minors!"

"Minors, hell!" said a voice behind us. "In El Salvador, there's only one kind of lady who goes unaccompanied to a bar!"

We turned around, and there stood the madman we'd met in front of the hotel. I had forgotten all about him. "Señoras," he said mischievously, "my presence here renders you respectable! Let me buy you each a drink."

"Thank God!" we said in unison.

"It's never a bad idea to thank God," grinned our benefactor. "But in this case, you should be thanking Scotty McTaggart, late of the Franciscan Order, now engaged for the greater glory of God in raising tomatoes."

"*What?*"

"I'm what you might call a community organizer. I try to set up income-producing enterprises in villages that have lost all their menfolk to the war. Tomatoes have been my one success among many failures. My idea, Señoras, is to corner the ketchup market!"

Our drinks came, delivered by a now more cordial bartender. "*Perdon, Señoras,*" he explained, "*si yo supiera que ustedes fueron amigos de señor Scotty. . . .*"

"You seem to be well known around here," I said.

"I've been here a long time," Scotty replied. "The people have learned I'm harmless. There aren't many harmless Americans left around these parts. They're all either spooks or soldiers wearing civvies. El Salvador is not the safest place these days for gringos. A lot of the locals blame Uncle Sam for the war. Me among them."

"Not many Americans around these parts, *period*," I said. "We seem to be the only people in this hotel, Americans or otherwise."

"Four people were gunned down here last week. Happened right out by the pool. Business has fallen right off since then."

"Who shot who?" I asked, trying to appear matter of fact.

"Don't know. Maybe a right-wing death squad knocking off suspected rebel sympathizers. Or else rebels knocking off rightists. I don't even bother to find out anymore." He grinned, mimicking a hayseed farmer. "Ah jes' raise tomaters, Ma'am."

I picked up on the act. "Shur' 'nuff," I drawled. "By the way. Ah'm Barbara, an' this here's my fraind, Lucinda."

"Pleased t'meetya, Miz Barbara. You an' Miz Lucinda both. An' what is it, iffen Ah kin ask, that brings you nice ladies down to these parts? It don' look to me like you's with the Go'mint. Course I could be wrong about dat. But somehow I don' believe you bes Go'mint types."

I hesitated. Sue had told me to expect hostility from some Salvadoreans who saw international adoptions as another form of gringo exploitation. I wasn't sure how Scotty would react but decided to level with him. "We're here," I said, dropping the hayseed act, "representing an American adoption agency. We've got six kids upstairs we're taking home with us."

"Good for you!" said Scotty. "Orphaned kids haven't got a snowball's chance in hell in this benighted country. So the more you take home with you the better! Anything I can do to help, just ask."

"For starters, you can tell us what in the world is going on down here!" said Lucinda. "We land at the airport, and there's no one else there but us and a million soldiers. Then our taxi driver gets roughed up by some punks in uniform on our way into the city, and now here at the hotel I could swear our phones are being bugged. I mean, I know they've got some kind of revolt going on, but that's supposed to be way out in the country. At least that's what we were told."

So Scotty told us about the war. He told us how for decades El Salvador had literally been owned and controlled by the so-called "Fourteen Families" and how in the early 1960s, peasant farmers, the majority of whom were tenants to these rich families, had risen up to demand land reform. He spoke of how the Catholic Church, which had once been part of the ruling oligarchy, had, after the Vatican II pronouncement, become increasingly vocal in calling for a more just society and how El Salvador's ruling junta had enlisted Uncle Sam's knee-jerk support simply by branding the peasant farmers as Communists. Armed guerilla resistance began in the rural countryside, and before long the struggle turned into a civil war. By 1984, the civil war had shifted from rural areas to urban centers.

"So there you have it," he concluded bitterly. "We, who should be supporting the folks who are fighting for the same things our Founding Fathers fought for, are instead supporting their oppressors. So you see, ladies, why it is that Americans are none too popular with the common folk down here."

He scribbled something on a piece of paper and handed it to me. " I got to go—I've still got a two-hour drive ahead of me tonight. If you do run into any kind of trouble, call this number and ask for Sister Marta. She's a nun and a friend of mine. She can probably help you."

"We leave in two days," I said. Will we see you before we go?"

Scotty didn't think he'd be back to the capital that soon. But he gave me his phone number in Washington, where, he said, he visited frequently trying to raise money for his work.

"Washington?" Lucinda laughed. "You sure *you're* not a spook?"

"Swear to God!" he grinned. "The seat of government is also the seat of the Franciscan Order. I still get a lot of help from the Franciscans. Ours was an amicable separation!"

With that he left. Lucinda looked at me with raised eyebrows. "Think he's for real?"

"I think if I was more religious, I'd have to believe God sent him to keep us out of trouble!"

*   *   *

What followed was a night of horror. A night of nonstop crying. A night of vomit and diarrhea. A night when our three-year-old went wild, crying for her mother and trying to escape. Neither Lucinda nor I slept a wink. Our only consolation, judging from the sounds coming from the adjoining room, was that the Lords weren't having it any easier.

By the time Margarita arrived the following morning, we were all red-eyed and exhausted. Our drill sergeant lined us up and explained the day's routine. "We will all walk to the court house. Yes? I will lead. You will follow with the children. All except Carmelita. She will walk with me."

"Thank God," whispered Lucinda.

Margarita did not break stride. "We will go to the second floor to the judge's antechamber," she continued. "You are only allowed on the second floor. You must stay exactly where I show you to stay. There are no bathrooms. So it is not good to drink so much coffee. Yes?"

She marched us off to the courthouse, which, providentially, was only two blocks from the hotel. All that morning we sat in the judge's empty antechamber surrounded by desks heaped with dusty papers. I recognized the ribbons and the stamp of the New York consulate on some of them. "So that's where they end up," I said disgustedly. "A lot of peoples' dreams sitting there gathering dust."

Our six little charges were by then so worn out they could only whimper. Sometime after midday a harried-looking woman appeared, spoke briefly to Margarita, and then closeted herself in the judge's chamber. "The judge has not come in," Margarita explained. "This lady is his secretary. She will act for him to perform the adoption ceremony. You will be called by the name of the child you represent. Yes?"

The Lords, as the only ones there who were acting on their own behalf, went in first and came back out hugging their little boy. "What happened?" asked Lucinda.

"We don't know," said Phyllis. "We had to raise our right hands and swear something in Spanish. I have no idea what it is we swore to, but it seems to mean that this little guy is ours now!"

After that we each went in and took the same unintelligible oath on behalf of the absent parent for whom we'd been given power of attorney. All went well until Peter, who was representing Julia's new mother, came back out shaking his head. "No go!" he said. "She says the papers are all screwed up. Julia can't go with us."

His wife jumped up, outraged. "Nonsense!" she said. "I'm sure it can be straightened out. Here, let me. . . "

Margarita planted her tiny self firmly in front of the taller American woman. "Sit down, Señora!" she barked. "You will only make things worse!" Phyllis sat down. "You will take the children back to the hotel," Margarita ordered me. "Señor Lord and I will remain here and see what can be done for Julia. Yes?"

We had learned by now to do what we were told. So the three of us went directly back to the hotel, fed the children, and waited. For me that afternoon seemed interminable. My own prospective child was to be brought by for me to see that evening, and it seemed as if evening would never come.

Peter and Margarita returned at five. "I guess it's okay," Peter said. "The judge's secretary says everything's now in order." Margarita seemed less confident.

By seven that evening, the tropical twilight was bringing a fleeting beauty even to the dismal shantytown outside our window. I was looking out the window, watching the sunset, when I saw a taxi drive up and two women get out, each carrying a white bundle. All of a sudden I found I couldn't breathe. My heart pounded against my ribs. I grabbed for the windowsill to steady myself.

So this is what it's like, I thought to myself. I'd had no idea the glimpse of a child not even yet my own would affect me so physically. I ran down to the lobby and met the women coming in. "*¿Cuál es Tamsin?*" I asked, so out of breath I could hardly talk at all. One of the women smiled and held up her bundle. Inside was a tiny brown child, only a month old and so emaciated she might have been a living skeleton.

I led the two women up to our room. The other child, a husky little boy, was a prospective son for a family in Worcester who wanted photographs of the child they had accepted sight unseen. I felt a fleeting tinge of envy, but then I looked again at the infant girl and realized I was already hooked. "My little brown chicken!" I whispered as I took the child in my arms. She was so small she seemed somehow transparent. I didn't dare squeeze her for fear she would break, but she looked up at me with calm, steady eyes.

Margarita came over, took one look, and put her hand on my arm. "She's too small," she said quietly. "She may not live, Señora." She turned and spoke rapidly with the women who had brought the child. I couldn't follow most of the exchange. Only that "*La niña es pequeña pero come bien.*" The baby was eating. So maybe there was hope.

Margarita was not convinced. "I can arrange to have the child seen by a specialist," she offered. "Then you can decide. Yes?"

Lucinda interrupted. "Barbara," she said urgently, "I think you'd better look at this little boy who's just come in. I think there's something very wrong with him."

I reluctantly gave up my little brown chicken and went to look at the other baby. He was a fine-looking 18-month-old, perfect in every respect except that his eyes never moved. I waved my hand in front of him. He didn't blink. His face remained expressionless. "Do you think he's brain damaged?" I asked Margarita.

"Maybe his village was bombed, Señora," she said. "He was very afraid. He is very afraid again now, but when he is no longer afraid he will be normal and his eyes will move. I have seen this many times."

The two foster mothers plainly were ready to leave. I took one last look at my future daughter and let them go. I was suddenly so tired I could hardly stand up. Margarita looked up at me kindly. "Tonight," she said, "your children will sleep at my house. And you will get some rest. Yes?"

As with all her orders, this one was not to be disobeyed. So Lucinda and I trooped across the street to Margarita's house and there put our charges to bed. Then we staggered back to our own room and collapsed onto our beds without bothering to undress.

The next thing I knew, the room was dark and someone was knocking on our door. I looked at my watch—10:30. What now? "Who is it?" I called groggily.

"Margarita," came the answer. "We have an *emergencia*, Señora. Pedro is unable to swallow. What food he tries to eat, it will not go down his *garganta*."

She opened the door. Margarita was also showing signs of strain. I had already noticed that this remarkable woman tended to mix up her languages when she was tired.

"I would have taken him to the doctor myself," explained Margarita. "But you have the custody now so I cannot. We will have to go together."

Peter came in from the other room. "Heard you talking," he said. "If you like, I'll come too."

"I have already called my nephew," said Margarita. "He drives a taxi and is a man who can be trusted. But it would be good to have another man, Señor. It is not a good hour to travel about the city."

Her nephew arrived 15 minutes later. We bundled up little Pedro and set off on a long drive through empty streets for the hospital. At one point Margarita pointed out a large official-looking building. "That is where Tamsin was born," she told me. "This is our Santa Teresa Hospital. On the other side of the building there is a long line of women waiting outside the maternity ward. Many times their children are born on the street before they get into the hospital. But Tamsin's mother was a lucky one. She did get inside."

"What happened then?" I asked.

"I don't know," said Margarita. "The mother is listed as a domestic in the home of a *funcionario*. Perhaps she knew she would lose her job if she kept the child. Perhaps she had other children to support. She would have to think about them. Yes?"

We continued on to another hospital, this one much more modern. The doctor in the pediatric ward, a handsome man I guessed to be in his mid-forties, spoke fluent English. "Where did you learn to speak like an American?" Peter asked him.

"Stanford. I did my residency there," said the doctor, plainly puzzled by this midnight visit from two gringos with a little Salvadorean boy. I explained the situation to him while he examined Pedro. "You're a lucky kid, Pedro, my friend!" grinned the doctor. And then, turning to me, "Nothing to worry about that I can see. I think what we've got here is a classic anxiety attack. I'll give you some phenobarbital to help him relax, and by tomorrow he should be fine."

Peter carried Pedro back out to the car. Margarita followed and I lagged behind. "Doctor," I asked him, "what would you say would be the odds for an infant girl who's nearly two months old now and still weighs only five pounds? Maybe even a little less."

"Hard to say without seeing the child," he said. "But if low weight's her only problem, she'll probably make it. If she's made it through her first month, she's probably in it for the long haul. Why do you ask?"

"I'm going to adopt her."

"I see. Well, you might think of it this way. She's already the survivor of a most brutally efficient kind of natural selection. No child who's born into poverty and pestilence is going to make it unless he or she is a pretty tough little human being."

"I hadn't thought of it that way."

"I have," he said sadly. "A lot. I'm not saying this process necessarily selects for what is best in human beings. It's not likely we're going to produce a race of artists and poets rising out of the gutter down here. But for physical resilience and natural immunities, give me any Salvadorean who's made it past his first six months any time!"

The doctor's beeper went off. He excused himself, and I went out to the car. We drove back to the hotel with Pedro asleep in Margarita's lap. Peter and I got out at the hotel. "Get some sleep!" Margarita called after them. "Today we must all go to the American Embassy. I shall have the children ready at eight. Yes?"

"That's one hell of a woman!" said Peter as we headed off to bed.

*   *   *

To get into the American Embassy, we had to pass through a whole series of checkpoints, the outer ones manned by Salvadorean soldiers and the one at the gate by U.S. Marines. Everything we carried except the childrens' papers was first searched and then taken away from us. "Why in hell search my briefcase if you're not going to let me take it inside anyway?" muttered Peter to the marine who was going through his papers.

"If we find a bomb in it," grinned the marine, "we shoot you first and *then* we confiscate your briefcase!"

That marine was the only person we met at the embassy with a sense of humor. We took our places behind a long line of Salvadoreans hoping to get out of the country and stood there all morning before a surly clerk called us forward one at a time to get the children's visas. Once again Julia's papers were declared not in order and once again Phyllis tried to bulldog the clerk into approving them. But this time Margarita, who must have figured we knew what to do in our own embassy, did not intervene.

The clerk called his superior. The superior studied the papers and called his superior. The superior's superior said they'd have to go back to the Salvadorean judge to get them reissued.

"We spent nearly eight hours there yesterday," raged Phyllis. "They told Lucinda everything was in order. There's no way we're going back there!"

"Then there's no way that child's leaving this country," said the official.

Lucinda and Margarita went back to the judge. The rest of us went back to the hotel. At three o'clock Lucinda returned, wearing an ear-to-ear grin. "We got the visas!" she yelled. "We can go home!"

I was happy for the other parents but sad at the thought that I'd have to wait another five months for my own little brown chicken's papers to clear.

We left for the airport at five o'clock the next morning to catch the morning flight to Miami. The terminal was still nearly empty except for armed guards and one woman who smiled at us shyly and approached us uncertainly. I recognized her as one of the foster parents who had brought the children to the hotel and was trying to remember which child that had been, when Julia, who had been holding my hand, tore free and ran crying into the woman's arms. I started after her but Margarita held me back. "Let them have a moment together," she whispered. "That lady is her mother."

"You mean her foster mother."

"No, Señora. Her real mother."

"No! You mean her own mother raised her for seven years and *now* is putting her up for adoption?"

"The child's father was killed and now the family has no money. The child has no future here. That is why her mother is sending her to America."

Julia's mother led her daughter back to where we stood. The little girl quietly put her hand back in mine and did not watch as her mother turned and walked away.

Choking back tears, I went to get our boarding passes. Lucinda took charge of the baggage. Phyllis stayed with the children, and Peter went off to try and retrieve his binoculars, which had been confiscated by customs when we arrived in the country.

I handed the agent our 12 tickets. The man took an eternity to process the lot and when at last he handed me back our boarding passes there were only 11. "We're short one," I said. "I gave you ten tickets."

"You gave me 11 tickets, Señora."

"Look, there are 12 in our party. I gave you 12 tickets."

The man held up 11 stubs, displayed like playing cards in a fan. "Count them, Señora," he said smugly. "There are only 11."

I didn't know whether I was going to cry or else strangle the son of a bitch. "Well you'd better damn well find number 12!" I yelled so loud that a couple of guards began to move over in my direction. But I had managed to rattle the agent. The manager arrived and the ticket agent launched into a torrent of Spanish.

"He says you only gave him 11 tickets, Madame," said the manager smoothly.

"He's full of crap, too," I shot back, now really angry.

The manager shrugged resignedly and spoke again to the agent. "Give her the ticket," he told the man. "*Yo le llamo al teléfono.*"

"I understood that, you lying son of a bitch!" I yelled at the agent, surprising even myself. "You had that ticket all along didn't you? You were going to call the person you'd sold it to. Right?"

The manager shrugged again. "You have your ticket, Madame. Now I suggest you go see if you can use that sharp tongue of yours to assist Mr. Lord. He is being detained at customs."

"Oh for Christ sake!" I ran down to customs and found a furious Peter surrounded by guards and bellowing in English at an official who plainly didn't understand a word he was saying. "Peter," I yelled, elbowing my way past the guards and grabbing him by the arm, "forget those goddamn binoculars! We've got to get out of here before they lock us all up."

Our flight to Miami was uneventful except for vomiting infants, and by then we were used to that. I spent the hours entertaining little Carmelita and thinking about home, about my family, and about a real night's sleep.

In Miami we took our place in the line marked for American citizens and were pulled out of it by an official who took one look at our six brown children and ushered us promptly into quarantine. "You're going to have to let one of us out," I told him. "We're out of food and diapers."

"Sorry, Ma'am. Nobody can leave this room until they've been processed."

By the time the last of the children had been processed through Immigrations, the last flight from Miami to Boston had already left. I was beyond caring. I called Sue to tell her we'd missed the last plane to Boston.

"You *what?* There's five families waiting for you at Logan!"

"Blame Immigrations."

"Oh shit!"

"My sentiments exactly."

So we spent another night of horror in a fleabag hotel where the airline had reluctantly put us up and arrived in Boston at two o'clock the following afternoon. Peter and Phyllis Lord had said their goodbyes before the wheels even hit the ground and were off that airplane in a blur. To my annoyance, neither Sue nor anyone from Making Family Connections was there to meet the flight. I stayed on the plane with the other children and Lucinda left to round up the waiting families. While we waited, I and the two flight attendants who stayed to help me out did what we could to make six filthy and exhausted little people presentable for their new parents.

We decided the easiest way for everyone would be to have the families come aboard one at a time to claim their children. The four infants went first. Then came Julia's new mother. I gave the girl a hug and felt her trembling with terror. "Lucinda," I whispered as mother and daughter prepared to leave, "why don't you walk off with them? It might be easier for Julia."

That left me alone with Carmelita. I'd grown very attached to this little girl, who seemed so wise beyond her years. I'd even fantasized about trying to convince her new family to give her to me. And now I had to explain to her in my halting Spanish that she was going to be leaving me for a new mother and father. Carmelita started to cry.

Lucinda came running back aboard. "Barbara," she called, "you'd better come. Julia's new mother is trying to get her into a snowsuit, and the poor girl's gone wild!"

I found the scene just as Lucinda had described it. Julia was hysterical and her new mother nearly so. "Julia," she was saying desperately, "it's very cold outside. You have to put on your snowsuit!"

I knelt down and tried to comfort the child. Julia was trying to tell me something between choking sobs. It took me some time to make out the words but finally I got it. I looked up at the new mother. "Julia's never seen a snowsuit," I explained. "She thinks you're trying to put her in a bag."

"But I told her it was very cold outside."

"She doesn't speak English."

"She doesn't? Nobody ever told me that!"

"Come on! You mean you don't know any Spanish?"

"Not a word. It's dumb, I know. I just expected she'd be able to understand me."

I had an inspiration. I explained to Julia that since she and her new mother didn't know how to talk to each other, she, Julia, was going to have to point to everything she saw and tell her mother what it was called in Spanish. Then in exchange her mother would tell her how to say it in English.

The little girl pointed to her suitcase and said "*mala!*"

"*Mala,*" said her new mother. "We say 'suitcase.'"

"Sooti case," said Julia, giggling.

I left them laughing.

I went back to the plane and found Carmelita's new parents, a minister and his wife from New York, already on board. The wife was very, very pregnant. She smiled a wonderful smile. "We didn't exactly plan it this way," she said. "We've been trying to adopt Carmelita ever since she was born. But she didn't have a birth certificate, and they wouldn't let her out. Then I got pregnant and here she comes! So I guess we're doubly lucky!"

David was waiting for me when I finally got off the plane for the last time. "You don't want to see me!" I grinned at him. "I've been peed on and thrown up on and I haven't had a bath in two days and I can't even stand myself!"

"You look pretty good to me!" he said.

∗   ∗   ∗

Sue called me the night I got home. "So how about it, Barb?" she asked. "Now that you've seen the other end of it, are you ready to go into the business?"

"I don't know, Sue," I said honestly. "What's more important to me right now is getting my little girl out of there as quickly as you can move the papers."

"I'm working on it," she said. "But I'm getting a lot of heat from the bureaucrats because I don't have that damned license. Make things a hell of a lot easier if you joined the firm. So think about it. Okay?"

I had been thinking about it. I liked Sue a lot. But I was worried about going in with someone who seemed willing to play so close to the edge. I knew Sue had helped a lot of people. I wondered if she had hurt a lot of others. Not intentionally, but out of just plain carelessness. My own experience with her hadn't been all roses. First there'd been the effort and expense of preparing those never-used papers for Guatemala. Then there'd been the promised little girl allegedly reclaimed by relatives.

On top of all that, I couldn't help feeling that Sue had used me a bit by sending me to El Salvador without at least some warning of what I was getting in for. Taken individually, these were all small things. But taken together, they added up to something I wasn't quite sure I liked. Still, it was an intriguing idea, teaming up with that whirlwind of a woman. In the end, I told her I would have to put that decision on hold until I'd gotten my new daughter out of El Salvador.

A month later, Sue called to tell me there had been a major adoption scandal in Texas. "Big-time stuff," she said. "Seems a bunch of U.S. agencies were conspiring with a Mexican ring to peddle the same kid to five or six different families. Lot of gullible people spent big money, and all they got for it was a picture, if they even got that."

"But that's horrible!" I said. "Poor people!"

"Poor us too, Barb. The Salvadorean government has used this Mexican thing as a pretext to put a freeze on all U.S. adoptions until the guilty are brought to justice. I mean, if that's not the pot calling the kettle black, I don't know what the hell is!"

"But I can't wait, Sue. I've got to get Tamsin out of there before she starves to death!"

"No way you're going to do it, girl. Not legally."

I hung up and sat numbly staring at the phone. My eye strayed to the scrap of paper that I'd hung up on my bulletin board and then forgotten all about. On it was Scotty McTaggart's number in Washington. Impulsively, I dialed the number.

He answered on the first ring. I blurted out my whole story, starting from that day in my kitchen when David and I had decided to adopt a child. When I was done, he was silent for a long time on his end of the line.

"I can't promise anything," he said finally. "I have some connections in the government. Might help if I called them. You never know."

"Thanks Scotty. I'd certainly appreciate anything. . . "

"But damnit!" he interrupted. "Can you imagine the kind off bastards who would take advantage of parents wanting children? What a world full of scoundrels we live in, Barbara!"

"It's not just the scoundrels," I said disgustedly. "From what I've seen, there's as much just plain incompetence as there is dishonesty in the adoption business."

"Got to be a better way!" said Scotty. "How about you and I start our own agency and do it right?"

That was the beginning of our partnership.

4

No jackals need apply

*D*AVID came into the house to find me by the phone laughing. He looked surprised. Ever since returning from El Salvador, I'd been tormented by the recollection of the tiny, malnourished infant girl I'd left behind in San Salvador. So I hadn't been doing much laughing.

"What's so funny?" he asked.

"Nothing really. It just seems that every character I've met recently wants to become partners with me in the adoption business. Latest one's Scotty. He's the ex-priest I told you about meeting at the hotel in San Salvador."

Some weeks later, David and I drove down to Washington to talk directly with this man whom I still hardly knew. We arrived after dark on an early spring night in 1984, got hopelessly lost, and after an hour of total confusion with a street layout that permitted ostensibly identical addresses in different parts of the city, we finally stumbled onto the nondescript brick building in which Scotty kept the sleeping bag, two pillows, kitchen table, reading lamp, and ancient Remington typewriter that represented the sum total of his earthly possessions.

The three of us dined that night at the corner deli and then returned to Scotty's spartan quarters to find two college students, Steve and

Suzette, who were also camped there before leaving for Guatemala to work as volunteers with one of Scotty's community development projects. "You four will have to work out who gets the pillow," Scotty advised. "I've only got two and one's mine!"

Instead of going to bed, however, we ended up sitting on the floor, gathered in a circle around Scotty's only lamp and talking far into the night. We talked of injustice and of the inequitable distribution of wealth and of how the United States could always be counted on to back the wrong horse in Central America. I felt like I was back again in the sixties, when I, too, still thought I could change the world. But I sensed in Scotty and his two young apprentices a greater pragmatism than I had then. These three weren't out to change the world. Only tiny bits of it. A sewer here. A tomato farm there. They were chipping away at the edges of the vast problems that my classmates and I had agonized over in the abstract. I found myself wondering how much more hope and happiness there might be in the world now if all the energy and idealism of the sixties had been funneled into the kind of work Scotty, Steve, and Suzette were committed to. Those three were tiny lights in a sea of darkness, and it occurred to me as I watched their animated faces swaying in and out of the dim glow from our one lightbulb that we *can* do an incredible amount of good if we don't allow ourselves to be overwhelmed by the sheer magnitude of the problems that surround us.

My watch read midnight. David was beginning to nod off. Scotty was just hitting his stride. "Time to get to work!" he announced, setting his typewriter on the floor in front of him. "Tonight we create an adoption agency!"

"Wait a minute!" I laughed. "Tonight we talk about the *possibility* of creating an adoption agency! I'm a burned-out social worker, and I'm not sure I'm ready yet for a new career."

"Okay," said Scotty, "we'll leave it in the conditional. We'll talk about what we'd do if we *were* running an adoption agency."

"First thing I'd do," I suggested, "is to charge our clients only what it cost us. It strikes me as kind of disgusting that people actually get into this business for the money."

"Agreed," said Scotty. "And we'd work only with others who are not in it for the money."

"Wish somebody had warned us about the people in it for the money!" yawned David. "We've already shelled out a bundle to the pack of jackals who orbit around the adoption business trying to get a piece of the action."

"No jackals need apply to this firm!" declared Scotty. "It will just be the two of us. Barbara handles the American end. She finds the clients. She gets the accreditations and the licenses. She does the home studies. I find the kids. I deal with the local authorities. I do the traveling. Agreed?"

"Wait a minute!" I protested. "You say I'm supposed to handle the business end? Hell, Scotty, I can't even balance my checkbook! And if I did become partners with you, my interest would be in the kids, not the paperwork. But I haven't said I would yet, remember?"

"Seems to me you haven't got much choice, Barbara," said Scotty quietly. "After all you've seen wrong about the adoption business, you can't just stand by idly and not try to fix it, can you? I mean, God's marching orders to all of us are that we leave things better than we found them? Right?"

Right, I almost said, but didn't. I wasn't sure what I thought. I'd never been particularly introspective. Whenever someone asked me what had led me from a privileged childhood into a career in social work, I'd always grin and give the same canned answer. "Guilt!" I'd say and change the subject. But I didn't entirely believe that myself. Guilt makes you do things you really don't want to do. And I really *liked* what I was doing. By giving something to others, I was giving something to myself. Maybe that's what Scotty meant by "God's marching orders?" I decided perhaps it was.

"Okay," I said, "I'll do it, Scotty! As long as you don't forget that God didn't equip this marcher with much of a head for paperwork. You're going to have to help me with those forms."

Steve was grinning at Suzette. "All this sound familiar?" he asked her.

"He hooked us on the same line, Mrs. Birdsey!" Suzette laughed. "Congratulations! You've just been recruited as another private soldier in General McTaggart's army!"

"God set the hook!" laughed Scotty. "Not me." He went to the refrigerator and came back flourishing a fifth of J&B. "A toast," he said "to the success of the firm of Birdsey and McTaggart!" He couldn't find any glasses, so we passed the bottle around the circle. There wasn't much left in it when Scotty announced it was time to get back to work.

"How about going to bed?" moaned David.

"Not before I exorcize my new partner of her demon," grinned Scotty.

"What demon?" I asked groggily.

"Fear of forms!" Scotty bellowed. "Paralysis in the face of unintelligible applications, written by bureaucrats trying to cover their asses and required in triplicate by agencies with imposing names!"

"Hallelujah!" shouted Steve. "Tell it to us, Brother!"

"Tell us *why* you tell it to us, brother!" laughed Suzette. "Accepting this Great Truth of yours doesn't leave us believers with any fewer forms to fill out!"

"No," admitted Scotty, "but it does alter your approach. Because once you recognize my Great Truth, you'll just fill out those forms with whatever nonsense comes into your head and send the damn things back! The trick is just to keep the paper moving!"

My new partner grinned a maniac's grin. "Watch and marvel!" he commanded. "Right now we are nothing. In the eyes of the law we do not exist. But by the time you sluggards wake up, I, Scotty, the Confounder of Bureaucrats, will have drafted up articles you can take to your secretary of state up there in Boston and get us recognized as a Massachusetts corporation. All I need from you guys is a name."

"Birdsey and McTaggart won't do," said Suzette firmly. "How about something with Guadalupe in it? Wasn't the shrine at Guadalupe devoted to motherhood?"

"Motherhood and family both," Scotty corrected. "But I'm partial to the name Hermandad. In Spanish *hermandad* means brotherhood. I'm superstitious enough to think the word might even have some magic in it."

"Then call yourselves Hermandad de Guadalupe!" laughed Steve. "You could translate that as 'Brotherhood of Motherhood,' which sure as hell should keep those bureaucrats guessing!"

So Hermandad de Guadalupe we became.

I fell asleep that night to the sound of Scotty banging out our bylaws on his ancient typewriter. One of the keys kept sticking, and, although it must have been just a dream, I thought I heard some very unpriest-like language coming from the kitchen.

*   *   *

The next day David and I drove back to the Cape and back to worrying about Tamsin. I tried to keep my mind occupied with the business of organizing my new career. Scotty's articles of incorporation sailed right through the secretary of state's office, and his application for tax-exempt status did likewise with the Internal Revenue Service. Hermandad de Guadalupe became Hermandad de Guadalupe, Inc., a charitable organization under the provisions of the IRS Code, Section 501(c)(3). All we needed now was a license from the state's Office for Children to start doing business in Massachusetts. I sent off for the application.

I probably should have worried more than I did about what this new venture would end up costing. But so far our start-up cost had been minimal. Scotty was already commuting back and forth to Central America, and so he simply took on Hermandad as yet another of his responsibilities while down there. My own investment was substantially more of time than money. Neither one of us expected a salary, and so we hoped to keep the cost to our clients only to what was needed to cover our expenses. My mistake, in retrospect, was to seriously underestimate what those expenses would be.

I was still waiting to hear from the Office of Children when Scotty called from San Salvador with bad news. A friend of his named Dora, a former government official whose job it had been to oversee all international adoptions, had found our papers. They were stuck in one of the city's district courts run by a judge who was adamantly opposed to American adoptions. The friend did not entertain much hope. "There's other children, Barbara," advised Scotty kindly.

"You don't understand!" I told him. "I'm not sure I understand either. How is it that I can love a little thing I've only seen once? But I do, Scotty! I want that child!"

In despair, I decided to call Sue Hampson. Sue and I were still good friends. I'd been a bit uneasy when I told her I had decided to go into partnership with someone else. But Sue had only laughed. "Just as well, Barb!" she'd said. "The vultures are beginning to circle around Ol' Sue here. Some sonofabitch Honduran lawyer I trusted with a lot of money took off with the loot, and now the folks who put up the cash want it back. Can't blame 'em, really, except that I ain't got it to give back. But don't you worry, hear? *Your* money's safe enough. My credit's still good in El Salvador, and one way or another I'm going to get you that little girl!"

I knew she meant it. But I also knew that she had meant equally well by the parents whose money she'd lost in Honduras. So I was prepared for the worst whenever I called.

"I'm still one step ahead of the law," Sue would tell me. "But the bastards are gaining on me! Slimy prick Honduran lawyer! Never trust a man, Barb! That's the moral of my story."

Sue was still in business when I called to report on Scotty's news. "That's bad," she said. "Maybe we'd better move those papers to another court, Barb. If we pick a district away from the city, we may not run into as much anti-American sentiment."

"Doesn't that put us right back to square one?" I asked. "Won't Tamsin's mother have to come in and start the surrender procedure all over again? What if she won't do it? What if we can't find her?"

"Worth a try. If we do find her, there's a lawyer down there who I might get to go with her to court if she's willing. He and yours truly had some wild times together, which he'd probably just as soon forget, being that he's a respected pillar of the community and all that. So, not to worry. When I say shit, he shits!"

I did worry. For a week I hardly slept. Then Sue called back. "It's all set!" she said. "You and you husband get your tails down to San Salvador pronto, before things get screwed up again."

*   *   *

Scotty made us reservations in a hotel run by a friend of his, and on June 18, 1984, almost four years after our odyssey had begun, David and I flew to San Salvador to pick up our child. This time it was David's turn to look astonished at the poverty, which had grown even worse since I had last visited the city.

What bothered him most was the disparity between the shanties of the poor and the mansions of the well-to-do, which stood like scattered islands in a sea of poverty. As we drove up into the city, we passed splendid red-tile-roofed *haciendas*, surrounded by high walls and guarded by ornate iron gates, through which we could catch glimpses of the beautifully manicured grounds.

"'Enclaves of affluence' is what Scotty calls those places," I said. "His theory is that walls are what people who can afford it build to shut out what they've given up hope of changing."

Later on we passed a rail-thin child driving an emaciated cow up a steep hill. It was one scene of many like it, but somehow that cow's bell ringing so merrily as the exhausted beast and child plodded forward made the scene stick in both our minds. "Poor kid!" I said. "Our own two children could no more imagine this world than they could imagine living on the moon!"

"Makes you wonder," said David. "Might do Chris and Karen some good to trade places with that boy for a bit."

We were interrupted by the taxi driver. *"Llegamos, Señor,"* he announced with a scowl of disapproval for the down-at-the-heels but clean establishment Scotty had booked us into. I gave him a large enough tip to restore his faith in Americans and followed David into the hotel. The owner, Scotty's friend, was expecting us. I was halfway across the lobby, already starting to say *"Buenas noches, Señor,"* when David caught my arm, shouting, "Barb! There she is!"

I whirled around. Sitting quietly in the corner of the lobby were two women. I immediately recognized the one carrying a little white bundle as the foster mother who had brought Tamsin to our hotel room five months before. I felt the same almost physical shock that had caught me by surprise that first time. I had to force myself to breathe as I raced across the lobby, leaving the startled hotelier standing with his hand out.

Tamsin's foster mother smiled a toothless grin and held out the bundle. I accepted that little package as if I were being handed a piece of fragile china. I parted the blankets and saw again that tiny face and those impossibly large brown eyes looking solemnly back at me. "You made it, didn't you, Niña?" I whispered. Then, remembering, I presented our new daughter to my husband for inspection.

"Kind of skinny!" he remarked, blowing a once-in-a-lifetime opportunity to say something memorable. But he was right. Tamsin had grown a bit but she was still horribly thin and lethargic—almost like a rag doll—and still too weak to hold her head up. I just stood there rocking her in my arms, overcome by emotions too complex to sort out, until the hotelier, who had joined our little group, cleared his throat politely to get my attention.

"The two señoras have been here many hours with the baby," he explained, introducing the second woman as the lawyer who was handling the adoption. Then, bowing, he led the four of us up to our room.

The scene that followed was almost identical to the one I remembered from my last trip. The lawyer sat on one bed with her papers spread out around her. The foster mother sat on the other bed, feeding Tamsin out of a bottle painted red. "Why red?" David asked.

The hotelier acted as our interpreter. "She says she has six children," he explained, "so she paints each bottle a different color. That way she doesn't mix up the formulas."

David, with his engineer's mind, found that a very clever system. "Does she color code the children to match their bottles?" he laughed. "I see that Tamsin's also wearing red."

I hadn't even noticed what Tamsin was wearing. I looked more carefully at the elaborately embroidered red mantilla wrapped around my child's head. "Why, that's beautiful!" I exclaimed. "Did she make that?"

Tamsin's foster mother smiled sadly and replied in a torrent of Spanish that I didn't catch.

"She did make it," said our interpreter. "It is red, not to match the bottle, but because red is the color that chases away the evil spirits. She hopes you will keep it always as something your daughter will have from her own country."

I felt my throat go tight, and I wanted to hug this woman whose sorrow it was to live in a country that could not care for its own children.

The lawyer, meanwhile, had finished comparing her papers with the ones we had brought. She stacked everything neatly in separate piles and looked up with a smile. *"Todo está en orden,"* she announced. The two women gathered up their things and started to leave. Tamsin began to cry. Her foster mother turned back from the door and picked up the child she had cared for from the day it was born. She wrapped the baby tightly in a blanket and laid her down on the bed face to the wall. The crying stopped.

Foster mother and lawyer left quietly, leaving David and me for the first time alone with our new child. We tiptoed over to the bed and stood for a long time side by side looking down at the pathetic little form that lay there so quietly. Tamsin at six months still had no hair. She still looked like a little brown chicken, still too weak to sit up without help. "They did the best they could for her," I whispered, as much to myself as to David.

Later that night, Dora, the former government official, came by to see us. She was a friendly, energetic woman who went over our papers again with a fine-tooth comb. "This used to be my job," she explained. "I was the representative from my government who signed off on all international adoptions." She didn't explain why she had resigned, and I didn't ask.

"You won't have any problems if you act fast," said Dora, handing us back our papers. "Go to your embassy tomorrow. Get your child's visa. Then get out of the country as quickly as you can!"

The next morning we did just that. We waited in the same long line I had been in once before at the embassy, but this time the official we met was a nice woman who took Tamsin's papers and told us to be back at three that afternoon to pick up her visa. We wandered around the local markets until mid-afternoon, pushing our new daughter in the stroller we'd brought with us. Smiling people stopped us in the street, pointing to our little girl and repeating "U.S.? U.S.?"

"Sí," I smiled. "U.S.!" We had been warned to expect hostility. We found the opposite. We were back to the embassy promptly at three. Tamsin's visa was waiting for us. We confirmed a flight for the following morning.

That night we had dinner with Dora, who told us why she had resigned from her government position. "One day," she said, "I got a call to go out to the airport and pick up an Indian child who had arrived unaccompanied on the flight from Miami. So I went out there, and there was this terrified two-year-old who had a note pinned on him from the couple who had adopted him. The note said, 'This child is not what we were led to expect. We are sending him back.'

"That," said Dora, "is when I resigned."

*   *   *

We were back at the airport the next morning at the crack of dawn. Tamsin slept in my arms while from across the waiting room a wealthy Salvadorean mother with a chubby Spanish-featured child stared daggers at the three of us. "Madame disapproves of blond gringo ladies with dark children," David laughed. Our plane boarded on time. We taxied out to the runway. There was a sudden jolt. We stopped, sat a while, and then taxied roughly back to the terminal building. "Oh Lord, not again!" said the Swedish businessman sitting next to us.

"Not what again?" David asked.

"Guerrillas must have shot out the tires! Happens damn near every time I leave here."

"Why just the tires? Why don't they blow up the plane?"

"I guess they just want to show us that this government you Americans are spending millions to prop up is a paper tiger," said the Swede.

*   *   *

Tamsin, David, and I arrived home to a house full of packing crates late on the night of Chris' 18th birthday. We had sold our house and were in the process of moving when we got Sue's call to go, so when we returned we weren't exactly set up for a new baby. But the next morning it seemed the whole neighborhood showed up bringing food, "baby stuff," and even, compliments of a good friend, a Cabbage Patch doll. Chris and Karen got to meet their new sister and were suitably unimpressed.

Then we moved to our new house in Bass River for a summer of mixed joy and sadness. The joy was in watching Tamsin begin to respond to her new surroundings. She was a picky eater and an erratic sleeper, so I spent many mornings watching the sun come up while feeding bananas and hot dogs to my new daughter.

Sadly, I could not share this joy with my mother. Shortly after we returned from El Salvador, she was diagnosed with terminal cancer and came home to spend her last days at our family place by the water in Centerville. No one loved children more than she, and it broke my heart to see her too weak even to hold her new granddaughter. She died in September.

Chris and Karen checked in with their new sister on the rare moments they weren't either asleep or off with their teenage friends. But David and I thoroughly enjoyed having a "little one" again part of our lives, and we developed a whole new circle of friends among other families with adopted children.

In between setting up a new house and caring for a new baby, I worked at setting up Hermandad de Guadalupe. Tamsin, fatter and happier by the day, was my incentive. At night, when I stood looking down at my sleeping daughter, I found myself thinking of other abandoned children and of other waiting families, and I'd feel almost guilty at my own happiness.

And so, with Scotty's injunction about how to approach applications from agencies with imposing names firmly in mind, I set out to get the license that would allow me to bring all those children together with all those families that wanted them. As required by the "Standards for the Licensure or Approval of Placement Agencies Offering Adoption Services," I produced evidence of financial viability, concocted out of thin air a cash-flow plan and a fee schedule, copied another organization's personnel policy, assured the Office of Children that all our records would be "legible, dated, and authenticated," and developed a "fair and equitable complaint policy" (also copied). Then I got on the phone to Scotty and nearly burst into tears.

"I've been working nonstop on this miserable application for two weeks," I wailed, "and I'm not even halfway done!"

Scotty was maddeningly reasonable. "Just keep plugging, Barbara. There can't be anything they ask for that we can't give them."

"Yeah? Well how about this one? Section 5.01 (4) says we've got to provide interim care for children who are between parents. Where shall we do that? Your place or mine?"

"Why not just ask a local foster-care agency to give you a letter saying they'll provide this service if needed? That would get us around that one."

"You're right," I said meekly. "I just didn't read far enough. Section 5.06 (2) says it's okay to do that."

"What'd I tell you?" he laughed. "You just got to be creative, that's all!"

"I am being creative. I've just put the Reverend Father Scotty McTaggart in charge of pregnancy counseling for surrendering parents!"

*   *   *

On one of my many frantic phone calls to Washington for help in the weeks that followed, Steve answered instead of Scotty. "Suzette and I haven't seen much of Scotty recently," he told me. "The General's got himself a girlfriend."

"Scotty has a *girlfriend?*"

"Yep! Name's Nancy. She's got furniture! You wouldn't recognize this place. Chairs! Beds! Plates! The whole bit!"

Nancy, he said, was a lawyer who had worked with migrant laborers in Florida and, before that, lived in Peru, where she collected textiles and crafts. She met Scotty when she came to Washington to exhibit her collection at the National Geographic Society.

"Sounds like quite a woman," I said.

"She is!" said Steve. "So damned organized she's even got Scotty running on time!"

*   *   *

One hot day in July, while Tamsin slept outside in her playpen and I was laboring over the license application, I heard the crunch of tires on gravel and looked out my window to see an ancient VW Bug come wheezing painfully up our driveway. The car stopped as if never to run again and out got Scotty, Steve, and Suzette. Nancy, as it turned out, was working and hadn't been able to come on the trip.

"We're looking for a school bus," announced Scotty without preamble. "We thought David might be able to help us find one."

"You drove all the way up here from Washington in that wreck of a car to find a *school bus?*"

"No, actually we drove up to see Tamsin. But we thought if we could find a school bus at the same time, we could kill two birds with one stone."

Tamsin, awakened by the sound of the Beetle's death rattle, started crying. They all gathered around the playpen to admire my bright-eyed little girl. "Amazing what food will do!" marveled Scotty.

"Amazing what love will do!" corrected Suzette.

"There's no shortage of love of in El Salvador," said Scotty. "What's missing is food."

"Enough!" commanded Steve. "It's a beautiful day. No arguments!"

David had joined us. "What's this about a bus?" he asked Scotty.

"We're looking for a school bus for Steve and Suzette to drive to Guatemala."

"Sweet God! There's got to be easier ways to get to Guatemala!"

"A town down there needs a bus. Only problem is we haven't got a whole lot of money to buy it with. Truth of it is, David, we haven't got any money at all. But you being mechanically inclined, we thought you might be able to help us find a junker that could be made to run."

So, the five of us, with Tamsin in my arms, climbed into David's truck and drove to a heavy equipment graveyard near Hyannis where, surrounded by defunct graders and bulldozers, we found the bus of Scotty's dreams. "What we have here," he rhapsodized when we first spotted this vehicle that had been painted with flowers and peace symbols by the hippies who had once lived in it, "is a bus with soul!"

Scotty climbed into the driver's seat. "Another sign!" he grinned. "God has left us the key!"

"Okay" said David. "See if God will make it start."

He did, but with the help of the battery in the truck. We bought it on the spot for two hundred dollars I donated to the cause, and Steve drove it back to our place on an expired license plate.

The next day Scotty, the Confounder of Bureaucrats, went off to persuade the Registry of Motor Vehicles to issue tags and title while David tuned the engine and the rest of us painted Guatemala's newest school bus with a color scheme that would have been the envy and admiration of its former owners. Scotty returned triumphant that afternoon, and we all gathered around for a ceremonial installation of the license plate.

"Is this a christening or a consecration?" asked Suzette.

"A christening," said Scotty. "I baptize this vehicle 'Tamsin's Bus' and commit it into the hands of God to deliver it safely to Guatemala!"

Steve and Suzette began their journey that night. God threatened to abandon them in Mexico. Tamsin's Bus was confiscated, and all would have been lost if Scotty hadn't prevailed on his network of Mexican connections to overlook various minor illegalities involving the operation of buses by those not licensed to do so. A licensed truck driver was dispatched from San Félix to pick up the bus, and Steve and Suzette finished their odyssey as passengers.

*   *   *

Scotty left not long afterwards on a scouting expedition to investigate sources of adoptable children in Central America. He returned in September, and he and Nancy drove up to the Cape to brief me on what he'd found. It didn't look good. The war was heating up dangerously in El Salvador. Honduras was out, because the official there in charge of government orphanages was opposed to the idea of sending children out of the country. Mexico was still paralyzed by adoption scandals.

That left Guatemala. "Guatemala isn't exactly safe either," Scotty warned. "You don't read much about it in the papers because the CIA has stayed out of it recently, but a civil war has been going on down there for nearly 30 years now. Usual story. Leftist rebels, mostly Indians, up against a right-wing government. Over a hundred thousand killed so far and no end in sight."

In this war, apparently, government troops could be a greater threat to foreigners than the rebels. But, if the downside of working in Guatemala was the risk of run-ins with trigger-happy militia units, the advantage was the support and friendship we could expect to find there from that remarkable woman, Juanita Bermúdez. Scotty explained that he had met Juanita years before, when he had helped her organize an effort to bring running water and a sewer to San Félix. "The *campesinos* trust her," he explained, "and they'll listen to her with a lot less suspicion than they will to the lawyers most other agencies use to find kids. She's the reason I think we should start in Guatemala. Once we're established there, then maybe we can expand into other countries. But let's start in Guatemala."

"Let's start by going to the beach!" said Nancy. "I didn't drive all the way up here just to talk business."

Scotty looked horrified. "My idea of hell," he said "is sitting on a beach! You two go. I'll stay here and read a book!"

I liked Nancy right away. With short brown hair and a huge smile, she was a California Girl, and like all California Girls she talked a lot with her hands and threw in a lot of *wows!* and *oh boys!* She and I spent that afternoon climbing around the sand dunes at Sandy Neck. We talked mostly of Scotty. "I guess I know him as well as anyone does," sighed Nancy, "but sometimes I think I hardly know him at all."

"I know what you mean," I agreed. "Whenever I get a 'yeah' or a 'well,' I know the meter's run out. That's his way of cutting off a conversation that's getting too close to things he doesn't want to talk about."

Nancy laughed. "He does occasionally let slip a thing or two. Sometimes he'll lie in bed and tell me stories about the people he's known and the things he's seen and the places he's been. So I pick up a bit here and a bit there. Sort of like putting together a puzzle. I'm beginning to see the picture, but there's still a lot of pieces missing."

"I don't even begin to see the picture," I confessed. "All I really know of my new business partner is that he was born in Scotland and raised in Queens. Only reason I know even that much is because I asked him about his accent!"

"I know he was the youngest in a family of five boys," added Nancy. "I know he wasn't happy in Scotland, although I'm not sure why. I know he loves New York and that his idea of a good time is to be in the middle of a huge crowd of people. I think that's ironic, don't you? That Scotty, this dyed-in-the-wool city man, has spent most of his past 20 years living in the hinterlands of Central America?"

"I guess if you're a priest, you go where they send you."

"More to it than that. He loves Central America. He went back there on his own to work as a community organizer after he'd left the Franciscans."

"Know why he quit?"

"He didn't quit the Church, Barbara! Scotty gave up his orders, but he would never, *ever* quit the Church. Could be he resigned because Rome doesn't allow priests to get involved in politics. But that's just a guess. The only thing he's ever told me is that everyone in his class of novitiates are either dead or have left the order."

We'd been climbing a steep sand dune. Nancy flopped down panting on the top of it, and we sat there, arms around knees, looking out across Cape Cod Bay. "That's Plymouth over there on the far shore," I pointed out. "Take away all the houses, and what you're seeing is pretty much what the Pilgrims saw when they landed here."

"Reminds me of another of Scotty's stories," said Nancy. "In the mid 16th century, Spanish friars and a contingent of Spanish soldiers entered the broad valley of what is now called Esquipulas, which at this time was territory within Honduras. According to more than legend, the Indians of the region would assemble in this valley every spring to render homage to their gods for a fruitful harvest with familiar symbols for corn and rain. The tribal chiefs asked these strange outsiders to show them the image of their gods. That night, with the use of balsa, which grows in the area, the friars carved a crucifix. The next day they paraded it among the Indians. The chiefs were astonished at the image of a man who was clearly suffering on a cross. How can you have a god that is bound and suffering? The friars explained that their one God sent his son to suffer and die out of love for man. This concept of a suffering god so astonished and moved the chiefs that they got rid of their gods and decided that every year they would come and give homage to this god who was willing to suffer for them. To this day, literally millions of indigenous people from all parts of Latin America come every year in Holy Week to give homage to what is now called "The Black Christ" (the corpus on the cross has blackened over the centuries from smoke and incense).

Nancy paused, looking out over the dunes, and then turned to me, smiling. "I wonder if that story has anything to do with why a Scot who came from Queens and loves crowds spent all those the years alone in the mountains of Honduras?" she asked.

5

She walked back up into the mountains

*L*ATE in 1984, Massachusetts revised its adoption regulations, making obsolete much of the work I had already done and leaving me in despair. Time spent at my desk was time spent away from Tamsin, and I begrudged every second of it. So I called Scotty and told him that my priority for the moment had to be diapers rather than paperwork. He seemed relieved. This joint venture of ours, hatched on the spur of the moment and carried forward at the start on a wave of initial enthusiasm, wasn't leaving him much time either for the myriad other projects from which he was finding it harder than he'd expected to extricate himself. We decided to slow down a bit. Scotty would continue to develop contacts in Guatemala as his schedule permitted. I would keep plugging away, and when it all came together, Hermandad would open for business.

Just as I was starting to tackle the new application, the mother of one of Karen's friends, a woman named Sandy Cohen, offered to help out. Sandy took over a huge table, made up labels for each section of the "Standards for Licensure," and listed the required "evidence of compliance" under each heading. So arranged, it became all the more obvious that the Office for Children's regulations had not been framed with international adoptions in mind. Procedures designed to insure

76

informed consent on the part of surrendering parents failed to take into consideration differences in language and culture. The kind of detailed information required to be furnished by adoptive parents concerning their prospective child was unobtainable in parts of the world where just keeping a child alive took precedence over maintaining "chronological records of developmental milestones." Elaborate pre-placement medical examinations of children prior to their adoption were hardly feasible. And in every case where compliance with the regulations was impossible, we had to file requests for waivers in which we would have to explain such things as why it would be difficult to involve the children themselves, even if of age, in the "placement process."

Sandy had the determination of a bulldog. I paid her part-time but she worked full-time and then some. We were a good team. Week after week, we worried at those interminable regulations while mountains of papers grew on her table documenting "evidence of compliance." Jill Harris, the agency caseworker assigned to monitor Hermandad's application, often seemed just as exasperated with the process as we were and did what she could to expedite action on the many waiver requests we submitted.

Even so, another year went by without the Office for Children's approval.

Tamsin learned to walk. I took her everywhere, and everywhere we went this lovely, alert, dark-skinned little girl was the center of attention. Most people just stared. Others were blunt to the point of rudeness. "Is that child really *yours?*" was a question I came to expect. I always answered yes.

We went to the bank one day, and the pleasant woman behind the counter couldn't keep her eyes off my daughter. I braced for the inevitable question, but it never came. "Wouldn't I love to have one just like her!" grinned the teller.

I told her something of the problems we had trying to adopt a foreign child and of my own long-delayed effort to set up an agency that I hoped could eliminate some of those problems for others.

"If you ever do get your agency off the ground," she said, "keep us in mind. My name's Cherie Dryz and my husband is Dan. We'd love to have a kid, but if it doesn't happen, that's okay too. Our life together is pretty full as it is."

* * *

In October of 1985, the Massachusetts Office for Children finally issued Hermandad a provisional license, and later that month Scotty, Sandy, and I flew to Guatemala City and then took a bus to Esquipulas. Sandy tells the story of that bus ride better than I could:

> "So after this hellacious flight through godawful thunderstorms we land on what seemed like the top of a mountain and the first thing that strikes me when we get off that airplane is the smell. It isn't a bad smell but it's . . . different. I mean, since I'd never been out of the country before and I wasn't expecting that the first thing I would notice is a smell. I ask Scotty about it and he tells me it's sewage and dead animals but mostly it's the wood fires, which are used to cook on.
>
> Next observation . . . armed guards everywhere. A rapid reminder that I'm in a country that's right up there in Amnesty International's Top Ten. But I'm not worried because I can see right off that Scotty knows his way around.
>
> "He gets us a taxi and we drive into the city to this Hotel Centanario next to the Government Palace. I'm suspecting I'll be getting up front and personal with those unfamiliar odors I first experienced when landing. Oh yeah, this is not getting much better and there's a drunk lying across the doorstep which forces us to climb over him while balancing our luggage and attempting not to appear unnerved by it all. "We're staying HERE?" I ask Scotty.
>
> "'We ain't in Paris, Honey!' he tells me. 'This place's got running water and a john, so count your blessings!'
>
> "My room costs three dollars a night. It's clean and it does have a john, which you're not allowed to put toilet paper into and the shower just runs a trickle but I'm too tired even to care.

"*The next morning we dine on Egg McMuffins! We're tourists with a capital T. On our way to the Golden arches, we pass shops with beautiful Guatemalan textiles and so when we get back to the hotel I attempt to cash some of my traveler's checks. Since the clerk doesn't have enough quetzals, Scotty directs me to the closest bank. 'Come straight back here,' he says. 'Do not pass Go!' and I am reminded again that this is not Cape Cod!*

"*That afternoon we took the bus to San Félix. Scotty has told us not to expect a Greyhound, but even so, the bus station is a shock. Kids, chickens, and dogs everywhere! Dozens of porters start scrambling around us and before I know what's happening all our bags have disappeared! But Scotty says not to worry. 'You haven't seen anything yet,' he tells us. 'Wait 'til you've been on that bus for five hours! Riding a bus is one of the best ways there is to get to know the real Guatemala!'*

"*He's right about that. Guatemalan buses are commonly referred to as 'chicken buses,' because they usually carry as many chickens as people. We go down the mountain, out of the jungle and into a desert. Jesus, it was hot! And every time we stop, which seeems often and somewhat of a mixed blessing, vendors jump on the bus and push Coca Cola! I mean, the country runs on Coca Cola! Straight up or laced with rum!*

"*Anyhow, we haven't gone too far before I realized my dressing faux pas. I'm wearing tight white pants which bear the last three hours worth of food, dirt, and animal stains. I'm sweating like a pig. The springs in the seat are poking into my butt, and I'm starting to get cramps and the ride from hell has just begun.*

"*I'm in a front seat. You know, your typical tourist! I want to be where I can see the sights. We travel out of the desert, back up into the mountains, going about a hundred miles an hour. The lanes are about as wide as my driveway at home with a drop of umpteen thousand feet on one side and sheer rock on the other. No guardrails! No nothing! Our driver seems hell-bent on passing every truck on the road. He has a spotter leaning out the right side window to see around the corners! I suppose that was a good thing or he*

may have hit one of the hundreds of white crosses which memorial-
ize the less fortunate fools that traveled this road before me!

"So there I am, sitting there, waiting to die, saying to myself
that this can't get any worse, when we come to this military checkpoint. Dozens of vehicles have been stopped and the guards are
searching every one of them. Everybody is shouting. Scotty comes
up from where he's sitting in the back of the bus and warns us to
say we are just tourists. 'You're going to get searched,' he tells us.
'Seems they're looking for some English woman who's got ties to
the guerrillas, so don't be surprised if they act kind of suspicious!'

"'Just what I need,' moans Barbara. 'And I'm probably the most
English-looking woman within a hundred miles of here!'

"'You got troubles!' I tell her. 'Here I am caught by an army of
fourteen-year-old soldiers with machine guns and I'm traveling
with a renegade priest and a woman who's a suspected English ter-
rorist. What will they do with me?'

"'Just show them your passports and let me do the talking,' says
Scotty.

"'You?' I say. 'Isn't this the part of the world where they like to
pop off leftist Catholic priests?'

"He just laughs. When our turn comes to be searched they make
us stand on a chicken crate and then this kid who couldn't have
been much older than my son begins patting us down, and I mean
he doesn't miss an inch! 'Just don't squeeze too hard, honey,' I tell
him in English, 'because I have to pee something awful!'

"We finally get back on the bus and I find my seat had been
taken over by roaches. Hundred of them, each one about as big as
my thumb. The other passengers are sort of snickering and waiting
to see what this gringo lady is going to do about those roaches, but
by then I'm beyond caring so I gave them something to laugh
about, say the hell with it and sit my ass down.

"So we start off again, and increase our speed to make up for
lost time. One of the men gets up and says something to the driver
and the driver stops right in the middle of a blind curve and every
man gets off the bus and pees down the side of the mountain. I

guess by then Barbara's teeth are floating too. But she has more nerve. 'Where do the ladies go?' she asks the driver.

"'Aqui!' he says, and makes the men all go back to their seats. Barbara gets off and does her thing right there beside the bus! I didn't have the nerve.

"The temperature on the bus must be one hundred and ten. The road we're on runs for a while along the Honduran border and we start passing Army tanks. Tanks for God's sake! I'm almost hoping one of the damn things will shoot us and put me out of my misery. But they don't, and finally the bus stops next to some ram- shackle buildings and Scotty says this is where we get off.

"The reward for surviving our bus trip lay ahead. We got to walk for a mile carrying all our roach-infested bags along a dusty road into the city, and that is how we got to San Félix."

*   *   *

We arrived on this first visit to Juanita's house right in the middle of a party she was giving for her graduating students. Children, parents, relatives, and friends were milling happily about, all turned out in ragged but spotlessly clean clothes. Juanita, tiny and radiant, wel- comed us in perfect English before being whirled away in a sea of laughing people. I was too tired after that bus ride to do much more than watch this extraordinary woman, whose grace and sparkle seemed to banish, for that evening at least, the poverty and hardship that were so obviously a part of those villagers' daily lives.

Much later that night the whole party moved to the neighborhood restaurant. The place was stacked, floor to ceiling, with wooden crates filled with the green glass bottles I remembered from when I was a girl. "So that's where they all went," I shouted over the din to Scotty.

"All *what* went?" he shouted back.

"Coke bottles!" I giggled. "Tanks and guns and Coke bottles! That's what we send to Guatemala!" I realized I was getting a bit in the bag.

"You better eat something," Scotty grinned. I asked for a ham- burger, and when an hour later it arrived, the nearest thing to ketchup

I could find was a bowl full of some unknown condiment, which I slathered onto my sandwich hoping that it might kill the taste, if not the smell, of a very suspect hunk of ground meat. I was too far gone by then to notice the silence that fell over the crowd as I took my first bite.

That unknown condiment turned out to be a pepper sauce hotter than anything I could have imagined. I howled and wept and choked and prepared to die. Everyone else tried not to laugh, but the effort was too much. The entire restaurant erupted into gales of laughter as Scotty pounded me on the back and José rushed up with a Coke to help put out the fire. So it was that I became an instant celebrity in San Félix.

Sandy and I slept that night at Juanita's house. Sandy could hardly bring herself to go into the evil-smelling, dark-tiled cubicle that was the only bathroom. "How do you flush this thing?" she gagged as I waited for my turn outside the door.

"With the bucket!" I hollered back. "Fill it up and dump it in!"

A long silence followed. "What's going on in there?" I finally asked.

"What's going on is that I'm filling the bucket like you said, but it's going to take me all night because the water's just dripping out of the faucet."

"Well, dump in what you've got and come out of there!"

Another long silence.

"Come on, Sandy! Move it! I'm so full of Coke I can't hold on much longer!"

"I dumped it in," came the despairing wail from behind the wall, "but it won't go down!"

*   *   *

The next morning we breakfasted on Coca Cola and then were taken by Juanita to meet the man who would be handling the legal side of our adoptions. "I picked this particular lawyer," she explained, "because he is a good man who once did a bad thing, and that has given him a social conscience." The story behind that "bad thing" was a sad one. Apparently when this lawyer had been a young man, his wife had caught him in an affair, and when she had confronted his mistress, the other woman had thrown lye in her face, leaving her blind.

The lawyer, when we met him, hardly fit the lady-killer image I had formed of him after hearing his story. He was a small, quiet man who seemed genuinely to want to help abandoned children. He shared the common reluctance to talk about money but implied that his fees would be only enough to cover his own costs.

We spent the rest of the day looking at old Spanish buildings and Indian women washing clothes in the river. "Just like those pictures in the travel brochures!" marveled Sandy.

"Hell, what did you expect?" grunted Scotty.

The only discordant note in an idyllic afternoon occurred as we were walking back into town. In the distance but drawing closer came the sounds of amplified male voices and firecrackers. I couldn't quite decide if these noises were threatening or festive.

"It's a political rally," Juanita explained. "My husband's party, but not," she added emphatically, "my own!" Trucks full of rum-flushed men firing guns and shouting into hand-held loudspeakers roared into sight. Juanita kept her eyes locked straight ahead as they went by. I think part of what I heard were insults aimed in our direction, and I began to realize Scotty had been serious when he'd told us that Juanita's progressive political positions put her at very real physical risk.

We spent our second night in the home of the expatriate American woman who years before had financed Juanita's training in the United States as a Baldwin teacher. Juanita's eccentric benefactor, whose last name I never learned, now had in her care a group of young Indian girls she also hoped to help. She was known only as Claudia, and she ran her house like a nunnery. The girls in her care wore white, slept in a common dormitory, and began each day by lining up and singing hymns outside the communal lavatory.

Sandy was in the shower when Claudia's morning service began. The lavatory had no door. Sandy had no dressing gown, and her naked, panicked dash down the ranks of lined-up worshipers only added to our fast-growing reputation as crazy gringos. Breakfast at Claudia's was also communal. We drank coffee brewed from whole beans boiled in a giant pot and sweetened with raw, brown sugar while giggling girls watched our every move. Claudia was apologetic about the shower. "Our water comes from the mountains," she explained, "and when there's no rain, there's no water."

That night we attended another fiesta, this one in our honor at José's house. One of the guests took it upon herself to teach Sandy Spanish. "Your friend is blond, so for her to speak Spanish is impossible," declared this self-appointed tutor, nodding in my direction, "but you will have no trouble!"

As the night wore on and the ratio of coke to rum grew noticeably less, I felt myself again getting lightheaded. I had to force myself to concentrate when Juanita took my arm and led me into a hallway where the noise from the party was somewhat less. Waiting there was a very patrician Spanish woman in the company of a tiny, wizened Indian mother clutching a ten-month-old child. Juanita introduced the taller woman as Rafaela Matos, the wife of the local coffee baron. The Indian woman she introduced simply as Dolores.

Dolores stepped forward timidly and offered me her child. "She would like you to take her baby," explained Rafaela in good but accented English. "Dolores has already had ten children. Most of them are dead. This is her youngest and she would like him to have a better life than she can give him here."

"Wait," was all I could think to say. "I'll go get Scotty and Sandy." I waded back into the party, not even realizing until too late that I was carrying the little boy. I found Sandy munching on a meat stick, and, before I could even explain what was going on, the child had grabbed that meat stick and stuffed it in his mouth. "Tough little bugger!" I laughed. "Come on, Sandy. This kid's going to be our first client!"

Scotty was nowhere to be found. Sandy followed me back into the hall, and, with Juanita interpreting, we explained to Dolores that she would have to go before a judge to surrender the child. Dolores nodded and smiled a wonderful toothless smile. "She thinks this one is an exceptionally intelligent child," explained Rafaela as the two of them got up to leave. "She asks only that you see that he gets a good education."

*   *   *

Sandy and I left the next day in a battered old pickup with two men from the village who had offered to drive us back to Guatemala City. We decided that even five hours jammed into the back of the cab was preferable to a repeat of that last bus ride, but we hadn't gone far before it became obvious that our two chauffeurs were looking for an evening's entertainment. "Tonight," said the driver, "we go dancing. Yes?"

They were gentlemen enough to take no for an answer.

We flew straight home. I was in the process of setting up a small family foundation with the money my father had left me and needed to get back to the paperwork. We had no reason to stay longer. We'd done what we'd come to do. That and then some.

*   *   *

When I got home, I called Cherie Dryz, the woman I'd met at the bank, to ask if she wanted a year-old boy. "Sure," said Cherie. "Boy or girl, it doesn't matter to us. As long as he's healthy, intelligent, and good-looking, we'll take him!"

I told her the whole story of that unexpected evening in San Félix.

Cherie was overwhelmed. "I thought they were all orphans," she whispered. "It just seems so *wrong* that a woman would feel she has to give up a child she loves."

I told her about my trip to El Salvador and how I watched a mother who had lost her husband say a final goodbye to her seven-year-old daughter. "I know what you're thinking, Cherie," I said sadly.

"But is it right for Dan and me to somehow *profit* from the fact that mothers have to make such choices?" she asked. "Is it right for us to accept this child, knowing he's being given up by a mother who loves him?"

I said I couldn't help her with that one.

She called me back later that same evening. "Dan and I have talked it over," she said. "We've thought about how we would feel to be parents of a child we weren't able to provide for, and we've decided to go ahead."

"We're novices," I warned her. "We'll do our best for you, but don't get your hopes up too soon. Okay?"

"Not to worry!" Cherie laughed. "We won't get obsessive about this prospective new son of ours."

That same day I began the mandated home study. Cherie and Dan, who were both active in amateur theater, were rehearsing at the time for *Man of La Mancha*, but I was able to corner them for long enough at odd hours to conclude that if ever there was an ideal couple to weather the stresses involved in an international adoption, it was the Dryzes. Dan, big and smiling with large, capable hands, was the engine shop teacher at the Upper Cape Vocational High School. Cherie had moved from her job at the bank to the local elementary school, where, despite a job title of secretary, she spent many of her own hours reading to the children, organizing plays, and in general making herself indispensable.

On the face of it, Cherie and Dan seemed not to have a care in the world. In fact, for all of their married life, they had been riding the emotional roller coaster of hope followed by disappointment common to all couples who are trying against all odds to have children of their own. They had endured an endless round of specialists and fertility clinics, and, in the end, when everything had failed and they were both approaching 40, Cherie wrote a poem she called "Requiem to a Lullaby":

> We knew we could have touched the sky
> But now we'll never hear you cry
> We really could have loved you best
> The babe who'll never suck my breast
> The seed that cannot come to be
> Although we struggled hard for thee
> A lullaby you will not hear
> Goodnight sweet dream, you were so near.

I watched with a mixture of amusement and concern as the two of them fought a losing battle against getting "obsessive" about the child they knew only from the photographs we'd brought back with us. "No harm in sending down care packages, is there?" Cherie called to ask, trying to sound matter of fact. "I mean, even if this does fall through, Adam can still use the stuff. Right?"

"Adam?" I asked. "Who's Adam?"

"Adam is what we've named our son."

I hung up knowing how much Cherie and Dan were going to suffer if I didn't get them their Adam. But everything seemed to be on track. The Dryzes' papers made their way through Immigrations, through the Massachusetts Secretary of State's Office, through the Guatemalan Consulate, and finally, all emblazoned with seals and ribbons, to San Félix. Juanita shepherded Dolores through the surrender process; José shepherded the papers through the courts, and, in March of 1986, the lawyer in San Félix advised us that all would soon be in order for Cherie and Dan to go to pick up their new child.

I called Scotty and Nancy with the news. Scotty was jubilant. Nancy less so. "It all looks too good to be true," she cautioned. True to form, Scotty offered to drop everything to fly down and see for himself.

I wasn't sure how Hermandad could pay for his trip. "Our out-of-pocket costs are already pushing the $3,500 estimate I gave Dan and Cherie," I told him. "We've paid Juanita $300, all of which she's spent on food and medical care for Dolores' family. José's $400 has gone to court costs, and I haven't totaled up what I'm out in filing fees and phone calls, but I know it's a bundle."

Scotty paid his own way. Once in San Félix, he walked through all of the courts and agencies the Dryzes would have to deal with to insure that all was, in fact, in order. It was. Juanita and José had done their jobs well. Scotty called me to report that all was well except for a small diplomatic problem that I had created by sending to San Félix a surplus computer I'd scrounged from the Digital Equipment Company. My idea had been for this machine to go to Juanita's school, but others in the town felt it could be better used elsewhere. The spokesman for this second group was an expatriate American friend of Scotty's named Jim Chadwick, who had married a Guatemalan girl, managed a San Félix restaurant, and become active in local politics. He and Juanita were often on different sides of political issues, and my computer had become another bone of contention between them. Scotty was caught in the middle. He'd thought to solve the problem by suggesting that the Dryzes stay at Jim Chadwick's home while they were in San Félix. But this tactic had offended Juanita, who had intimated in her soft spoken way that if the Dryzes were going to stay with Jim Chadwick, then Jim Chadwick might as well meet them at the plane and escort them through the entire adoption process. That is how matters were left.

*   *   *

On the sixth of April, 1986, Cherie and Dan left for Guatemala City. Years later, while Adam and his younger brother, Jesse, slept upstairs, they sat in their living room and reminisced with me about the journey they'd made to get the first of their two sons:

DAN: What was it like? Well, we came in at night, and I looked at the city and there were almost no lights, and I thought, "Uh-Oh, I've seen that before." I guess it was because I'd been to Viet Nam, and I knew there was also a war going on in Guatemala, so I had sort of the same feelings when we landed.

CHERIE: I was scared too. Dan had been to Europe as well as Viet Nam, but I'd never even been out of the country… And I don't like to fly!

DAN: Jim Chadwick met us at the airport.

CHERIE: He didn't have any trouble finding us. I mean, we *stood out!* I'd bought a new dress because I wanted to make a good impression, and on the plane trip to Miami I spilled spinach all over it! So when we landed in Miami, I ran to the only place I could find, which was a gift shop, and I bought this silly T-shirt with flamingos all over it, and I thought, "Oh my Gosh, when they see me wearing this thing, what *are* they going to think?"

DAN: If she'd known she'd be wearing that same foolish shirt for the next three days, she'd really have freaked! But that's what she did. Because they lost our luggage. Jim said we couldn't do anything about that until the next day, and so we went on to the hotel.

CHERIE: Our hotel was just across from the National Palace, and the National Palace had just been car bombed.

DAN: Troops everywhere you looked.

CHERIE: Seeing all the military with their rifles! I was *so* afraid...

DAN: I was more worried about our hotel room. There was water all over the floor.

CHERIE: That wasn't important to me. I wanted to be a good ambassador, not be complaining all the time.

DAN: She didn't want to be the Ugly American! But we sure as hell were the Ugly Smelling Americans! We wore the same clothes our entire stay in Guatemala City. And, believe me, it *was* hot! For two days we followed Jim from one office to another trying to track down our stuff.

CHERIE: Jim was always very diplomatic. I was very impressed with his manner, but I wasn't used to how things are done down there, and I got kind of frustrated. I mean, all this talk and nothing was *happening!* And then everywhere we went, there were those soldiers with guns! I felt like freezing whenever I saw those soldiers. I remember I smiled so much! I just *smiled,* and I sort of tried not to *move* too quickly.

DAN: We never did get our bags in Guatemala City. The airline finally shipped them to us at San Félix after Jim had driven us out there.

CHERIE: That ride in Jim's car had to be the worst! I remember looking at the speedometer and seeing 100 miles an hour and Dan trying to tell me those are not miles, Cherie, those are kilometers, but it didn't matter, we were going too damned fast for those tiny little roads!

DAN: I remember as we got closer to San Félix on the highway, you could see where they dumped their garbage. Huge dump on the top of a hill right outside the city.

CHERIE: The smell! I'll never forget that smell!

DAN: Jim had told us he was a member of the San Félix Chamber of Commerce, and I thought to ask him why the hell they didn't do something about that garbage! But then we went a little ways further along and there was this overlook, and we got a beautiful view of the Cathedral.

CHERIE: That *was* beautiful! But all the hills around the town were bare.

DAN: We did that. American timber companies cut down all the forests. They were trying to replant them when we were there, but a lot of people made a living cutting firewood, so you can see the problem.

CHERIE: Then we drove down into the town, and we spent that night at Jim's place.

DAN: The next day we met Adam. We were sitting in Jim's restaurant waiting for Dolores and getting panicky, thinking maybe she'd had a change of heart.

CHERIE: Then we saw this Indian woman walking down the street, and she was carrying this screaming baby, and I was saying to myself, "God, I hope that's not the one!"

DAN: But it was Adam. Dolores had brought two of Adam's brothers with her, and we bought them all ice cream.

CHERIE: And it suddenly hit me. This is our *son!*

DAN: Well, he wasn't ours yet. We still had to see the judge.

CHERIE: Somehow I had the feeling Dolores was glad we were getting Adam. Probably just wishful thinking on my part, but, I mean, what a lovely woman! She had the most beautiful eyes! I was glad too that we were the same age. She was 43 at the time, and I was 40. I was glad she wasn't, say, 18.

DAN: That whole meeting was really kind of surreal. Jim translated for us. We tried to tell Dolores how happy we were. She thanked us for the ice cream, and then she and her kids all got up. Dolores just picked up Adam and said goodbye and walked back up into the mountains.

CHERIE: The next day we started the adoption process. The first thing we had to do was to drive out to the county courthouse to arrange for a social worker to visit Dolores. I was terrified. The day we arrived, Jim got a bomb threat, I don't know what it was about. Something to do with the Chamber of Commerce trying to move the vendors away from the Cathedral. Whatever it was, every time I got in his car, I just *knew* it was going to blow up!

DAN: We ended up making four trips to the courthouse. First trip, we had to *arrange* for the social worker. Next day Jim had to drive us back again to *pick up* the social worker and then take her to Dolores' place. No way you could drive up to where Dolores lived. I don't know how Jim got as close as he did. He took that little Datsun places I wouldn't have taken a Jeep!

CHERIE: Then we got to where we had to walk. We were climbing this really steep hill, and I was worrying about Jim because he's got a bad heart, and when I tried to make him rest he laughed and said, "If I die here, Cherie, I'm that much closer to touching heaven!" And I thought, "My God, that's right out of my poem!"

DAN: When we finally got to Dolores' little one-room adobe brick hut with its open cooking fire inside and this one big iron pot and her kids all over the place, it still seemed to me like some kind of a dream!

CHERIE: That's just what I felt. I had to pinch myself to make sure I *wasn't* dreaming!

DAN: We had to wait again in San Félix for the social worker's report, and when finally we got that, Jim drove us back to the court for the third time to get final approval for all the papers.

CHERIE: Our appointment with the federal registrar was at ten in the morning, and when we got there, right on time, he wasn't there. We waited what seemed like hours outside that office until finally Jim sat down and typed out our papers himself!

DAN: Whatever he did must have worked, because the next day we went before the judge for the adoption ceremony. Dolores and Adam weren't there. I think that made it easier for everyone.

CHERIE: That was April 15, 1986, and what I remember best about that day is Jim turning to us as we walked out of the courtroom and saying, "He's yours now!"

DAN: And I remember you saying, "He's ours *and* Dolores'." Because that's the way we wanted it to be.

CHERIE: Dolores was going to meet us at noon, but we waited until two o'clock and there was no sign of her. "She can't do it," I was saying. "She can't give him up!" And then we saw her walking toward us down the road carrying Adam. Dan took Adam, who wanted ice cream, and I hugged Dolores, and I couldn't let her go. I wanted so much to be able to say to her in Spanish what I was feeling, but all I could say is, "We will love him! We will love him!" and every time I said it, Dolores just hugged me harder.

DAN: We watched Dolores walking back up that mountain until we couldn't see her any longer, but she never looked back. Then Jim drove us to Guatemala City, and along the way we stopped at a little store that had a single gas pump and music blasting from a loud-speaker. And I just looked at Cherie because they were playing the soundtrack from *Man of La Mancha!*

CHERIE: Can you believe that? They were playing "The Impossible Dream"! The same song that had meant so much to us during all those years when we were trying to have a child of our own! That *had* to be more than a coincidence!

6

The hard part is just beginning

*H*ERMANDAD de Guadalupe never advertised its services. We got as many referrals as we could handle by word of mouth. And we wanted to stay small. Scotty and I agreed that the day we became so large we were no longer able to get personally involved with each one of our clients would be the day we packed it up.

Most of our cases began with a phone call. It was usually the wife who called. "I understand you do adoptions," would begin the uncertain voice on the other end of the phone. "Could you tell me something about your agency?"

"Yes," I'd say. "We're a very small, very new service on Cape Cod. We can arrange direct adoptions from Guatemala, and we can also help with independent adoptions from other countries." If my caller was new to the game and not clear on the terminology, I'd go on to explain that with direct adoptions our agency would actually locate the child, while with an independent adoption, we would do the home study and help with the rest of the paperwork while the prospective parents would use their own sources to find a child in whatever part of the world they chose to look.

Usually, however, the people who called me were not newcomers to the game. They knew the jargon, they knew the frustrations, and they knew the disappointments. I learned to expect suspicion. Most had been burned before, and I couldn't blame them for suspecting that I too might be one of the sharks. So I'd tell them of my own experience with Tamsin, and that would usually open the floodgates to the often tearful recitation of similar tales of hopes dashed and money lost.

"I know," I'd say at the end of these sad outpourings, "I've been there myself. Why don't we sit down together and see if there's a mesh? No feelings hurt on either side if it doesn't work out, okay? We're sort of like a large, informal family here, and we only work with people who are comfortable with us, and us with them."

And so the couple would arrive, the wife visibly nervous and the husband equally so, but trying not to show it. My heart always went out to them. I knew how desperate these two people were to make a good impression. When I'd worked for the state agency, I'd known insecure colleagues who had been drawn to social work because of the power their position gave them over indigent clients, and I'd seen the same thing again among some adoption agency staff members, who played on the vulnerability of couples desperate for a child. So the first thing I'd always tell prospective clients was that for my agency to be a success, I needed them every bit as much as they needed me.

Not every family was well suited for the arduous task ahead of them. I learned to recognize the danger signals, or "red flags" as we called them. One of the most common red flags was misguided altruism. I remember one couple who already had several children and told me breathlessly how wonderful it would be to adopt a poor foreign child who would otherwise never have all these great opportunities they were able to provide for their own children. I told them that was not a good reason to adopt a child. I asked them how they'd feel if they'd grown up being reminded, even indirectly, how fortunate they should think themselves to have been rescued from their own home and family. And I told them also that they were mistaken if they expected gratitude from the people they met in whatever country their child might come from.

Another red flag I learned to look for was differing levels of commitment. I recall talking with another couple and being halfway through my spiel about the difficulties they could expect to encounter in the course of the adoption process when the husband looked at the wife and said, "See, honey? I told you this wasn't a good idea!"

I let them argue it out, and when finally the wife turned to me and said, "Don't worry, he'll come around," I told them if they weren't together at the start, there was no way they would be able to pull together during the tough times ahead.

I was just as firm with couples who were obviously unrealistic in their expectations. And as time went on and I saw more families who were willing to go through the fire, I found it harder to stay patient with those whose commitment was more shallow. Couples from off the Cape who announced glibly that they were "down for vacation and just thought we'd check it out," couples from on the Cape who came to Hermandad "because it beats having to drive all the way to Boston," and couples who were plainly comparison shopping for the lowest fees all got politely shown the door. So did the families who hadn't done their homework. But if a husband and wife could tell me, "we've been to the meetings, we've heard the problems, and we still want to adopt," then I was confident we could work together. Those who hadn't yet reached this point I referred to the Latin American Parents Association, the Open Door Society, or another organization offering various meetings and workshops to prospective adoptive parents.

Some people just wouldn't listen. One older couple about whom I had real reservations was so insistent on finding a Latin American child that I took Tamsin when I visited them. The gentleman and his matronly wife watched in horror as my little hellion laid waste to their impeccably furnished cottage, and by the time I finally reined in my daughter, they'd decided that an adopted child was not for them. "Good Heavens!" said the wife as she walked me to the door, "I had no idea Indian children were so *dark!* Whatever are you going to do when she's older and doesn't get invited to birthday parties?"

Race certainly was another red flag. I made sure everyone thought through the implications of adopting a child of a different skin color. "No problem!" most would assure me. "Perhaps not for you," I'd answer. "But how about for other members of your family? Are you sure there aren't others, perhaps from your parents' generation, who would be upset at the idea of a dark-skinned child, not biologically related, carrying the family name?"

It was a constant surprise to find couples who had never considered that a child from another country wouldn't be just like the child next door. "If you really want a Caucasian child," I'd tell them, "your best option is a domestic adoption, and those we don't do. But be careful. There are a lot of con-artists in the white-baby market, just as there are in every other market where buyers are desperate and demand exceeds supply."

The prospective clients I was saddest to turn away were those who hadn't yet abandoned the hope of conceiving a child of their own. Often we'd be approached by couples who were still going to fertility clinics, and I came to recognize what a draining experience that ordeal could be, both emotionally and physically. For husbands especially, trying to start the egg in a glass jar could be totally demoralizing. So if a couple came to me who were still trying to conceive a child of their own, I'd suggest to them that even if they could stand the emotional strain of trying both approaches at once, it would not be fair to the child they might adopt. Their commitment had to be there to *that* child, not as a backup, but as the baby they really wanted.

Parents still ambivalent about whether to adopt or else continue trying to conceive I put in touch with RESOLVE, a national organization with an office in Belmont, Massachusetts, whose mission is to help those confronting the possibility that they might never be able to have children of their own.

Some red flags were more subtle than others. Sometimes I'd see a couple who just seemed wrong to me. I couldn't quite put my finger on why, but I would know during that first interview that it just wouldn't work. My intuition would tell me that they weren't going to support each other, that there would be fighting when the going got rough, and that the best favor I could do them was to discourage them from the idea. That is what I tried to do.

With everyone who came to see me, I began by emphasizing the negative. I'd much rather have said how wonderful it all was, but I had to tell them instead that this would be the hardest thing they would probably ever go through in their entire lives. I'd tell them about Julia's mother, and that the child they might get could well be given up by another mother who made that sacrifice so that her baby could have a better life. "When you adopt a child from another country," I'd remind them, "you're not doing anybody a big favor but yourself. And if you're *not* doing it for yourself, you're not doing it for the right reason."

If they were still game, I'd go on to explain that Hermandad worked primarily in a relatively small area in Guatemala and that the parents there who agreed to surrender their children have no feelings about secrecy. They would want to know about, and if possible even to meet, the families to whom they were entrusting their babies. "So ours," I would say, "are usually about as close to open adoptions as is possible, given that the biological parents live in a foreign country."

To those not familiar with that term, I would explain that in an open adoption the parents meet, often prior to the birth of the child, and figure out whether they like each other, and, if it's a go, the surrendering mother and father will say, "Yes, we think you'll be able to do a better job with our child than we would at this point in our lives, *but* we're not willing to give up contact entirely." So a deal is struck, usually with an agency as intermediary, stipulating that the child will know both sets of parents, and visitations, or at the least written correspondence, will continue between them.

Some of my prospective clients rejected that idea outright. The possibility of an arrangement where biological and adoptive parents remained in contact was to them just wrong in principle. "It's not fair to us," one would-be father objected, "and it would not be fair to our child. He'd be pulled in two directions, and we'd just be setting him up for the temptation to bounce one set of parents off against the other."

I reminded him that *any* adopted child could play that game, whether or not he knows his real mom and dad. All he would have to say, and at some point certainly *would* say, is "I wish I had my *real* parents."

"When you hear that," I warned, "it's going to hurt. You want him to be all yours. You don't want anyone competing for his love. But the truth of it is he's *not* all yours."

"I guess what scares me," said one woman, "is that if I meet the biological parent, then I have to admit that there is somebody else out there who was really a part of my child's life. And my worst fear, of course, is that maybe someday that parent will come back."

All I could tell her was that perhaps when she actually got down to San Félix and saw the place and met the people, she might find herself wanting to stay in touch with her child's biological parents. And as to the possibility that those parents might show up again sometime in the future to hit her up for money or some such thing, the only insurance I could offer was to say that Juanita, who represents us to these families, spends a lot of time with each of them explaining that theirs is a gift that once made could not be taken back.

I did tell my prospective clients that they would take on one long-term financial commitment in Guatemala. I asked that every family who signed on with Hermandad consider sponsoring one child at Juanita's school, at a cost of one hundred dollars per year. I told them this was one way to retain a permanent relationship with the country that in a sense they would also be adopting. Very few objected.

Usually, when I had finished my "shock-couples-into-reality" approach to our first interviews, there would be a long silence, and then one or the other of them would grin and ask if there were any more unpleasant surprises I'd neglected to mention.

"Just one," I'd say. "The uncertainty is what will get to you most. If you're pregnant, it's a certainty. Sure, you can lose the child, but at least you're pregnant. There's something visible, something there to carry around with you, something that society accepts and understands. But if you're adopting, you have nothing. When you tell your friends you're adopting a child, that doesn't mean anything. Adopting who? what? when? where? It's all out there, floating around somewhere. It might not even happen. So you've got that awful vacancy, which only gets worse the further into this process you get. And you're all alone with it. People who haven't been through the same thing just can't understand what you're going through.

"Then one day I'll hand you a picture and a description of the child that may become yours. That's when I'm going to lose you. Because suddenly it *is* real, and you won't want to hear me telling you about all the obstacles that still stand between you and your getting that child. You're going to bond to that picture, and that is when you're going to be the most vulnerable. I tell you this only to warn you that you may *not* get that baby in the picture. I promise you, I won't show you a photo until I'm reasonably certain we can deliver, but nobody in this business can make guarantees. If they do, don't trust them!"

And if, after all my warnings and horror stories, those two people could still say to me, as one couple did, "Yes, we know. But we've been married seven years. We know we can't have children of our own. We've accepted that. We have a real interest in other cultures, and we think this is something we can do and do it well," then I'd know we had meshed.

*   *   *

Even so, I never took a commitment on the spot. "Go home," I'd advise. "Think on it some more and then call me back." I'd give them samples of the intimidating forms they would have to fill out and a phone number of someone who had already been through the ordeal and information about parent support groups. No matter how resistant my more reticent clients might be to getting involved in those support groups, I urged them to do so. I'd tell them it's a big world out there and, before they committed themselves to something as all consuming as an adoption, they needed all the information they could get.

Most couples went home, did all the things I asked them to do, and called back to say they still wanted to go ahead.

The next step, which was an awkward one for all concerned, was the home study. I explained that I had to determine, on behalf of the Commonwealth of Massachusetts, the Immigration and Naturalization Service, *and* the relevant agencies in the country from which the adopted child would come, if the couple in question were "physically, financially, emotionally, and morally" fit to be parents. My loyalties in this process were necessarily divided. It was as if I were a lawyer called on to represent equally both the couple who had staked so much of their future happiness on my ability to find them a son or daughter and also some still-unknown child whose own future happiness depended on the suitability of the parents to whom I would entrust it.

The couples I evaluated were also pulled in two directions. On the one hand, they would be desperate to make a good impression on me, this relative stranger who came into their lives as judge and jury. On the other hand, they couldn't help but resent that they, who had already invested so much in having children, had to be evaluated as potential parents when others, more fortunate biologically, could, as one bitter husband put it, "just crank them out."

I always addressed that resentment right off. "Look," I'd say while sitting for the first time in a living room obviously made spotless for my benefit, "I know that having some strange lady come into your house to pry into your lives is no fun at all. You just have to keep reminding yourselves that the objective justifies whatever embarrassments and inconveniences and disappointments you meet along the way. Think of what I'm putting you through as adoptive parents' labor pains!"

Then I'd go on to emphasize the importance of being entirely up front with me. "Big Brother's watching!" I'd warn. "They're going to run a criminal records check on you, and if you claim no record and one shows up it could queer the whole deal."

One husband I worked with had been arrested in college for trashing the ROTC office. "If that's going to disqualify us," he asked, "wouldn't I do better not to mention it and hope it slips through?"

"No," I said. "If they booked you for breaking and entering, that charge is going to appear a lot less serious if we can explain that it occurred during a peace demonstration than it would if it surfaced unexplained."

"Okay," he agreed, "but let's talk worst case. Let's say we reveal everything and you decide we don't measure up. What then?"

I told him that according to the law that would have to be a team decision involving at least two licensed social workers, whose decision could also be appealed.

I never saw that happen. Most of the time, what I learned in those home studies about our clients' backgrounds reinforced my belief that the adoption process was by and large self-selecting. It took good, well-balanced people to want to adopt a child in the first place. But even the most decent people revealed real difficulties. If one or both prospective parents seemed somehow too detached from their own extended families, I smelled possible trouble. "I haven't spoken to my parents in years," one man confessed.

"Why's that?" I asked. "Do they live far away?"

"Didn't used to. But I dunno. Maybe they've moved." I let that one go by, but later in our conversation he revealed that his parents had been fire-and-brimstone fundamentalists who made him so fearful of having unclean dreams that he was afraid to go to sleep.

I saw such an expression of pain flash across his wife's face as he told that story that I sensed a more profound problem. And when I steered the conversation to their efforts to cope with infertility, their palpable embarrassment at discussing this issue confirmed my suspicions. So I suggested as gently as I could that their own discomfort with issues of sex would make it hard for them to help their own child confront those questions when he or she became a teenager.

The husband reluctantly accepted the idea of therapy as "another hoop you're making us jump through to get a baby." His wife called up later to thank me. "How much happier our years together would have been," she said, "if only we'd done this sooner!"

The manner in which couples answered my questions was often as important as the substance of what they said. If either husband or wife dominated the conversation, or interrupted constantly, or corrected constantly, I'd make a mental note to touch on this when I interviewed each one separately. "Whatever tensions exist between you now," I'd warn, "chances are they're going to get worse once you have a child, particularly an adopted child. So for God's sake, say what you're thinking! If you get it out in the open now, it won't come back to haunt you later."

I spent a lot of time in our clients' kitchens and workshops, trading recipes, admiring home-built projects, and discussing the relative merits of Ford versus Chevrolet trucks. I walked through rooms already made over into nurseries, and laughingly investigated the adequacy of the plumbing. "Your water's not hot enough!" I'd announce, coming out of some too-tense couple's bathroom. "Sorry! You fail your home study! The whole deal's off!"

"*What?*" they'd cry, not entirely sure if I was joking.

"Says so right here in the regulations. Section 5.08(1)(b)(3) under 'Physical Requirements for the Adoptive Home': 'The adoptive family home shall have hot running water.' That's the law. So what can I do?"

But I could never look solemn enough as I tried to string them along with this foolishness, and we'd all end up relaxed and laughing at the absurdity of so much of what we were going through together.

Gradually, over the period of many interviews, I got to know my prospective parents pretty well. I asked them to look analytically at their own mothers and fathers. How had their parents raised them? What would they do differently with their own child?

We talked about jobs, goals, and priorities. About attitudes towards race. About their neighbors' attitudes towards race. About their expectations for this child of theirs, and how they'd feel if he or she ended up marching to a different drum. "What if Carlos doesn't *want* to be a violinist?" I'd ask, and they'd have to think about that.

About religion: Did they go to church? Was it essential that their child share their beliefs? If the biological parents requested it, would they object that he or she be raised a Catholic?

About finances: Could they really afford this child? Had they stopped to consider what the addition of another family member would cost them? Were there grandparents willing to help share the burden?

About recreation: What were their hobbies? What did they do on vacations? Would having a small child tagging along crimp their style? Would they resent having to give up or postpone doing those things they'd have to give up or postpone if they had a child?

About morals: What values did they consider most important? What did they feel was missing in our society? Who were their heroes? Why were these people their heroes? What kind of role models would they hope to be for their child?

About discipline: How had their own parents disciplined them? How well had these techniques worked? Would they use the same techniques with their own child? If not, what would they do differently?

About infertility: Even knowing I was rubbing salt into old wounds, I had to bring this subject up. There must have been hurt and pain, and if this didn't come out, I had to dig for it, because I knew it *would* come out at some point later, and I knew it would have an effect. So if they'd tell me, "Oh, it's no problem. We know we can't have children, and it doesn't bother us any longer," I'd say, "That just doesn't sound right. It's *got* to be a problem!"

"*Nobody* understands!" one wife wept. "We've never had anyone we can talk to about this goddamn curse of ours. Our friends get uncomfortable if we even mention that we've been going to a fertility clinic. My husband's mother hasn't exactly come out and said so, but I know she thinks I haven't done right by her Johnny. 'All my other daughters-in-law have had such *nice* children,' she tells her friends, 'and I'm sure Johnny's kids would have been *just* as nice if only Judy didn't have her problem!'"

It was no easier for an impotent husband. "The guys joke that I'm shooting blanks," confessed a burly construction worker. "So I laugh. I mean, they're my friends, those guys, and they don't mean nothin' by it. But even so, I sometimes feel like puttin' their fuckin' lights out!"

The trick was to get both partners talking. I wanted to hear them say, "Yes, we've gone through this. We know what it's like, and it's miserable. It's something that will always be with us. We'll always have these memories, but we feel we can put them behind us well enough to raise someone else's child as our own." But I knew how hard it had to be to say these things, particularly for a woman. Because what she is really saying is, "I can accept my imperfection. I'll never have this feeling of wholeness that I would have if I could bear my own child, but I can live with that. I can be a mother without looking at my child who is from a different place and wishing that I had given birth to him myself and that he *looked* like me."

"Of course I'm going to wish those things of my adopted child," said one woman. "How could I help it?"

"It's a slippery slope," I warned. "It's just so much easier for the person who has already had children to say 'It's okay. I can feel the same way about this adopted child as I can about my own.' But if you've never had your own child, how can you compare? How can you avoid the guilty feeling that somehow you're not giving your adopted child as much love as you would if he'd been your own?"

"You tell me," she persisted. "How can I?"

"I can't," I replied. "That's why I raised the issue. I wanted to alert you to these potentially corrosive doubts beforehand, and to tell you, for whatever it's worth, that as the mother of both biological and adopted kids myself, my feelings for all my children run just as deep."

*   *   *

Once these interviews were over, I had to write up the home study. It was not an easy job. Like so many bureaucratic requirements, the original purpose, which was to make a candid assessment of the couples' suitability as adoptive parents, had been in a sense subverted by the fact that anything short of an absolutely glowing report from the social worker could torpedo the entire process. If anything even slightly controversial came out, someone in Immigrations might flag it or some antagonistic reviewer in the country providing the child might kick it back.

My job, as I saw it, was to sell my clients to often skeptical buyers. So I would make my own private judgment, and if I thought the couple I'd evaluated would make good parents, then I wrote them up stressing their positive qualities every bit as far as honesty would permit. I exercised the option of being selective in what I included. I learned also to be sensitive to different cultural perceptions in the countries where my reports would be read. Knowing that mothers who worked could be suspect in societies where the woman was expected to be a homemaker, I would make a point of emphasizing a working mother's domestic qualities. "She loves cooking, baking, keeping house, and caring for children," I rhapsodized perfectly truthfully about one business executive, and, if all that wasn't enough, I went on to point out that she had "recently begun work on her first quilt."

Divorce, equally, was a ticklish issue in places where marriage vows were still considered binding. I tried to describe my clients' former marriages in terms designed to emphasize the impossibility of continuing the earlier relationship. The terms "agnostic" or "atheist" carried with them so much more baggage in Latin America than at home that I would write up clients who had so described themselves as "intensely moral individuals who do not belong to any church."

All this I did with a clear conscience. My responsibility was to pick up the loose ends as I went through the home study. If I found some issue that I felt needed attention, it was my job to help my clients get that issue resolved so that by the time we were done, they were ready to adopt. So the last thing I wanted to do was to throw them an unintended curveball because of some careless wording in their home study.

My clients rarely recognized themselves in what I wrote about them. "That's *us?*" they'd marvel. "After all the stuff we told you, that's *still* us?"

"That's you!" I'd say. "The All-American Couple! And I mean it, too. I think you guys are going to be wonderful parents to some lucky kid."

My All-American Couple would have been working on the rest of their paperwork while I'd been writing up the home study. They'd have their form I-600A, "Application for Advance Processing of Orphan Petition," ready to file with the INS. They'd have been to their local police station to be fingerprinted on form FD-258. Their "Criminal Offender Record Information" check would have come back indicating "No Relevant CORI." They would have assembled three copies of their birth certificates and marriage certificates, all with raised seals and signatures; three copies of their police clearances, medical reports, and IRS form 1040s, all notarized; three letters of recommendation, also notarized; and, finally, two photographs of each of them, one formal, the other casual, both signed on the reverse. They would think the hard part was behind them.

"It's not," I'd warn them. "The hard part is just beginning. The hard part is the waiting and the uncertainty."

*   *   *

In the fall of 1985, I had to live with an uncertainty of my own. In my case, the uncertainty was about Hermandad's viability. With our provisional license now in hand, inquiries from prospective parents were pouring in. It soon became clear that we could not remain the mom-and-pop adoption agency we'd originally planned. We'd have to grow both to ensure that we could continue to find kids for our clients and to earn enough fees to cover our operating expenses... even with Scotty and me receiving no salaries

The agency looked larger on paper than in fact it was. I'd printed up stationery on which, under an impressive letterhead and a rather awkward motto ("Helping Unite Many Through Direct Adoptions"), three office addresses appeared; one for my own home in Barnstable, the second for Scotty's apartment in Baltimore, and the third for Juanita's school in San Félix.

Scotty, now married to Nancy, had settled in Baltimore, where he had taken a job with the city and on his off-hours did the home studies for clients who came to us from the Washington-Baltimore-Philadelphia area. I called him one night at home to discuss the future of our joint venture. "We're getting a lot more inquiries from potential clients than we can possibly find kids for as long as we limit ourselves to just San Félix," I told him. "I've got some leads in the Philippines that I think we'd better check out."

"Go for it!" agreed my mercurial partner, and I realized I was on my own. Scotty had seen his role as helping me start up the agency and establishing our contacts in Central America. Now, with a family to think about and bills to pay, he found himself for the first time in his life needing a paying job. We left it that he would continue on paper as my partner and continue to offer help and advice whenever I needed it.

I was on my own. It was a scary prospect but made less so by the knowledge that Scotty would always be there if I had to call for help.

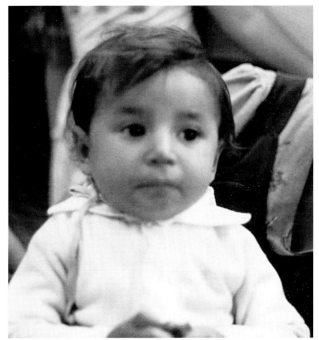

Adam the first time we saw him

Scotty greets an adoptive family returning to the United States

Steve, Tammy, me, Suzette, Scotty, and Dave on Cape Cod before "Tamsin's Bus" departs for Guatemala.

Adam (on rocking horse), Tammy, and me

Tammy in Mexico when she was five

Tammy becomes a U.S. citizen, assisted by Dave and me

Barbara and friends outside San Félix

Tammy, grade 10, at her high school's Jr./Sr. Prom

7

Treated as just another charlatan

$\mathcal{M}$Y introduction to the Philippines had come in a round-about way. Sandy Cohen had an uncle who had a friend who had another friend, an expatriate Philippine attorney named Francisco Lacuna, whose family maintained ties with the Marcos regime. Lacuna's cousin was an official in the Philippine Ministry of Health. Francisco had left Manila to establish a practice in Virginia. Sandy had heard a rumor that Lacuna was interested in arranging adoptions of Philippine children by American families. She passed this news along to me, and I called Lacuna and arranged a meeting at his Virginia office.

Francisco Lacuna was tall, middle-aged, sophisticated, and gen-uinely concerned about the plight of Philippine orphans. He explained that he needed to affiliate himself with a licensed American agency in order to arrange adoptions to the United States from Manila, and he was candid in admitting that his motives were not entirely philan-thropic. He was aware that there was money to be made in adoptions, and he hoped to expand his practice through this new initiative.

All in all, he seemed like someone we could work with. We met a sec-ond time and agreed in writing on respective responsibilities and fees. Lacuna would arrange for all the necessary legal requirements of the

Philippine government and would guarantee that all children made available would be legally free for adoption. Hermandad, on its part, would guarantee to provide qualified families to present as prospective adoptive parents and insure that they were properly prepared for the adoptive placement.

Lacuna suggested that I visit Manila with him to get to know the people with whom we would be working. At first I hesitated to commit myself to so long a trip at a time when I had so much unfinished business at home. But Lacuna was adamant. He warned that many Filipinos strongly resisted the idea of sending their children out of the country and urged that I go in person to demonstrate that I was sensitive to his country's traditions and committed to insuring that the adoptive parents with whom I placed Philippine children wouldn't allow them to forget their own heritage.

I agreed to go, even though the political situation in the Philippines was at the time fast disintegrating. Ted Koppel of ABC's *Nightline* had triggered the growing crisis when, during an interview with Ferdinand Marcos in the fall of 1985, he had asked the increasingly autocratic president when he intended to hold elections. Secure in his own invulnerability, Marcos replied that he would call an election as soon as he got home. To everybody's amazement, he did. Election day was set for February 7, 1986, a date Marcos clearly hoped would not give the opposition sufficient time to organize. But Corazon Aquino, wife of the martyred Benito, fooled him. She'd made her candidacy contingent on her supporters gathering one million signatures on a petition urging her to run. Aquino campaign workers took to the streets; the yellow ribbons that were to become the symbol of her crusade blossomed everywhere; and even before I first met with Lacuna, Marcos was already clearly in trouble.

I followed these events in the headlines and wondered how they would effect my own plans. Then one late-December day, while I was preparing for both Christmas and my upcoming trip to Manila, a friend of mine told me about a doctor she knew in Providence, Rhode Island, named Alex Sanders who had received his medical training in the Philippines and was married to a Philippine woman. My friend thought he might be willing to give me some insights about what I was likely to encounter in Manila. And that is how I first crossed paths with the man who was to figure so dramatically in my immediate future.

I called Sanders. The voice on the other end of the phone was brusque and confident. Sanders advised me strongly against going to Manila before the elections. He said Marcos "was finished," his government was in chaos, and anyone I met in the Ministry of Health if I went over in January would be out of a job after the elections the following month.

I asked him how he could be so sure Marcos would lose the election. His answer intimated inside knowledge. He reminded me that the Filipino community in New England was close knit, that the Aquinos (he spoke of them as "Benito" and "Corey") had lived not far from Providence during the years of their exile, and that he and his wife had known them well.

I told him of my arrangement with Francisco Lacuna and of the latter's insistence that I get to Manila sooner rather than later.

"Lacuna's part of the Old Order!" snorted Sanders. "If you team up with him and Corey wins the election, you're going to be associated with all the corruption of the Marcos regime, and your chances of arranging adoptions from the Philippines won't have a snowball's chance in hell!"

I thanked him for his advice, hung up the phone, and told David what Sanders had told me. David's advice was that I not dump Lacuna without giving him his day in court. He reminded me that Lacuna and I had signed a contract that might not be easy to get out of, even if Sanders' predictions were correct.

Lacuna was more amused than annoyed when I called him to express the concerns Sanders had raised for me. He explained how the Philippines had always been governed by a small number of prominent families who, no matter what happened, always ended up still running the show. "So don't worry!" he laughed. "We Filipinos do occasionally shuffle things around at the top, but when the smoke clears, you'll still find most of the same old faces behind the same old desks!" His advice was that going to Manila during the elections would actually make the trip safer. Why? "Because half the international press corps is in Manila covering the campaign. Right now security is tight. But after February that could change."

* * *

Sandy and I left for the Philippines on New Year's Day 1986. Twenty-eight hours later we landed stiffly in Manila's International Airport, where the first thing we noticed was that everyone in authority seemed to be wearing Marcos T-shirts. Attorney Lacuna, who insisted that we call him Paco, was there to meet us. Sandy asked him about the number of Marcos supporters. "If you're not for Marcos," he grinned, "you don't work at this airport!"

We drove down wide avenues lined with magnificent buildings to the Manila Hilton, where Paco left us that evening with the warning that the Philippines was a major supplier of Caucasian women to the Arab white-slave market. We weren't sure if he was joking.

In any event, we didn't take his advice to remain on the hotel grounds. After showers and a nap, we went out to see the sights but soon turned back. Manila after dark, we discovered, was a very different place from the sanitized city we had driven through earlier that afternoon. Under every bridge, in every culvert, in doorways, and gathered around trash cans, we found ragged street people staring dully at us or muttering sullenly as we passed by self consciously. "My God, Barbara!" whispered Sandy, "where do they keep them all during the day?"

"I don't know," I whispered back, "but I have a feeling we're more likely to end up in a morgue than a harem if we don't get our asses back to that hotel in a hurry!"

We didn't sleep much that night. "Those people out there all seemed so *alone*, Barb!" said a very shocked Sandy "Even in the worst *barrios* in Guatemala, you could sense some feeling of community. Here, even the starving little children seem solitary and desperate!"

* * *

Paco met us in the morning and took us on a whirlwind tour of government-run orphanages and urban redevelopment projects. The orphanages were clean, crowded, and impersonal. The redevelopment projects all appeared somehow too good to be true. At one, an impeccably neat skills-training center intended to teach sewing, Sandy, who herself likes to sew, immediately spotted the absence of cloth scraps and thread ends, which would have indicated works in progress. And at an attractive low-income housing complex, the families in residence looked so little like the street people we had seen the night before that I mentioned this to Paco. He said something to the effect that the government was understandably trying to put its best foot forward and then changed the subject.

The following day Paco left us in the charge of a social worker from the Ministry of Health, who took us on a tour of the city's historic sights. We visited the opulent cultural and trade centers, finding the first of these filled largely with Marcos family memorabilia and the second largely empty. Later that afternoon, in front of an old Spanish ruin, we were approached by a tiny girl and her even-smaller brother who silently held out their hands palms up in the universal plea for money. Both children were filthy, but dirt could not disguise the huge oozing welt on the little girl's face. I asked her in my halting Spanish how she had hurt herself, but the child gave no answer.

Our guide tried to hustle us along. "Wait!" I protested. "We can't just leave this child with that terrible sore. Ask her what happened to her face. Find out her name and where she lives."

The exasperated social worker spoke kindly to the child and then more bitterly to me. "Her family came to the city two weeks ago looking for work," she explained. "They live with another family in a truck under a bridge. The sore on her face is a burn. She has others on her back."

As if on cue, the little girl turned around and pulled up her shirt to reveal a great mass of raw, oozing welts. "She says her stove exploded, which may or may not be true," continued the social worker. "Parents sometimes disfigure their children to make them into more appealing beggars. From the way she shows off her back, I think that's probably what happened to her."

She looked at me, shamefaced. "You asked for her story, Mrs. Birdsey, so there it is. And please don't ask me what I can do about this situation, because I can do nothing."

"But isn't there someone in the ministry you could speak to?"

"There is, but nothing will happen except perhaps to make trouble for you. If you want to help this girl, give her some money and let her get on with her begging. Begging is less demeaning than prostitution, which is her other option."

*   *   *

We spent our last day in Manila with Paco at the Ministry of Health. We visited with a number of officials, though it was never quite clear exactly who was responsible for what. Everyone was cordial and everyone applauded our efforts to find American homes for Philippine children.

Everyone, that is, until we got to the office of the one official who really counted. For our last interview, Paco, looking uneasy, introduced us to Luisa Berino, director of intercountry adoptions. I knew that Paco's cousin had briefed Berino on why we were there and did not expect a hostile reception. But it was plain enough, as soon as we walked into her office, that Berino was not glad to see us.

I began, as I had with every other official we had visited, by offering her the small presents (in this case, bath soap) that Paco had advised us were expected by Filipinos receiving visitors or clients. Berino, a small woman who radiated large authority, smiled thinly.

"Wouldn't petitioners offering gifts to a public official be looked on somewhat suspiciously in Washington?" she asked.

"Paco briefed us on your local customs," Sandy volunteered brightly. Berino's smile evaporated. I realized with a sinking heart that we'd just dug ourselves into a deeper hole but saw we could do nothing else but to press on. I showed the director my resume, the fee schedule we and Paco had worked out, a statement of our agency's operating philosophy, and Hermandad's Office for Children license.

Mrs. Berino picked up the license. "This says 'Provisional' on it. What is a 'Provisional License'?" she asked.

I started to explain that in Massachusetts all new agencies were initially issued provisional licenses, but I was nearly drowned out by loud voices coming from the outer office. "Could we close the door?" I asked. "It might be less noisy if we did."

"Is there something you'd rather not say with the door open?" said Berino sharply, and I suddenly understood the reason for the almost palpable tension in that office. The director wasn't happy to be seen in the company of one of Marcos' cronies at a time when she wanted to put some distance between herself and the people who were about to get the sack. No wonder she didn't want to close the door!

I put four client files on Berino's desk. "If you'll look through these applications that I am submitting to you officially," I said in growing desperation, "I think you'll be convinced of my agency's qualifications. Everything included is exactly as specified in your guidelines, and all the papers have been certified by your consulate in New York."

She rifled through the folders while we waited uneasily for her reaction. When it came, it was ambiguous. "This couple," she said, "they're too old to adopt an infant. They'll have to accept a child of two or more years."

"I don't think they'd object to that," I said, relieved that the application hadn't been rejected outright. Berino nodded toward the door to indicate that our interview was over.

"Unpleasant isn't she!" muttered Sandy once we were out of earshot.

"She can be difficult," Paco agreed. "A stickler for regulations!"

"But if our applications are in order and our clients acceptable, then she *will* approve them, right?" I asked him.

Lacuna shrugged.

✳   ✳   ✳

We flew home the next day. Two weeks later, I got a letter, obviously drafted by Luisa Berino, but signed by her boss Ina Sanchez, Marcos' minister of health. Sanchez expressed serious reservations about the qualifications of Hermandad, citing five areas of concern: *first*, the agency's provisional license; *second*, the fact that Hermandad's application form for prospective parents made information about the clients' religious beliefs optional; *third*, that the home-study format contained no reference to the prospective parents' interest in Philippine culture or motivation for adopting a Philippine child; *fourth,* that the proposed fee structure was exorbitant, particularly in view of the fact that many of the services budgeted for in Lacuna's retainer were performed at no cost by the ministry; and *fifth,* that no mention was made of the Hermandad staffs' professional qualifications.

"*We generally do not work with newly organized agencies,*" the letter concluded, "*as we are concerned with the stability of the agency to ensure the protection of the Philippine child. We suggest that we consider your request after you have a permanent license and your agency is more stable. We hope that you only include mention of the Philippines in your brochure after our approval of working with you.*"

I stayed up all night composing a rambling reply to this letter, which reflected my surprise, my irritation, and my exhaustion when I wrote it. First I addressed the fact that Hermandad had prematurely issued a brochure citing the agency's ability to arrange Philippine adoptions. "*Our impression [from researching the ministry's own literature]*" I wrote " *was that as long as an agency was qualified to operate and the parents had met all agency, state and federal requirements in this country, then there was no reason that an application could not be filed with your ministry. . . . We were totally unaware of the apparent necessity for pre-approval of our agency prior to offering our parents the opportunity to adopt [a Philippine child].*" To this I added a zinger that probably further antagonized Berino. "*I must add,*" I said in reference to my meeting with the director of intercountry adoptions, "*that if there were any concerns at the time of our visit regarding our being allowed to submit applications for parents, I think these should have been raised at the time. . . . I consider this a matter of professional courtesy, especially considering the distance we had traveled.*"

Regarding our license, I pointed out that Hermandad operated under the "*very same regulations with a provisional license as we will with a regular license*" and gave Jill Harris' name at the Office for Children as someone whom the ministry could confirm this point. To the objection that we left our clients' statements of religious belief optional, I replied that "*we feel that the ethical and moral standards of the individual per se are more important than adherence to a particular church or religious belief."* I did add, however, that *"we do honor the particular requirements of the country to which we send documents, and will be glad to provide whatever information is required."*

I promised in future home studies to comply with *"whatever information and/or verifications the ministry may require."* As to fees, I pointed out that *"prior to our visit. . . we were unclear about the amount of legal representation our applicants would need before a child could leave his country of birth. We were both surprised and pleased to learn that no court expense is involved in the Philippines and that everything is handled on a very reasonable basis directly through the ministry."* In light of this, I agreed to set our fee for Philippine adoptions somewhere between $4,500 and $5,500 per child, which was to include the cost of travel/escort services and post-placement follow-up.

I went on at some length about the qualifications of the Hermandad staff. *"When our board of directors first met to establish this agency,"* I wrote, *"we made the decision to keep our agency very small and personal so that we could know and work with each of our families well. I am confident that the people who have come together for this purpose are not only truly caring individuals, but also fully qualified, both educationally and in experience."* That said, I listed the specific qualifications of our staff, pointing out that neither Scotty nor I received a salary for our work as co-directors.

I couldn't resist ending this six-page essay with another jab at Berino. Apologizing for my letter's length, I wrote, *"We feel it is of vital importance for us to clarify any misconceptions that might be held about our agency. We only wish that we could have met with you as Minister personally to address these issues at that time. . . . It is unfortunate that there is a lack of communication between what the Ministry requests from an agency and what is actually made available [to that agency] in the written material [you provide]."*

It was not a very tactful letter. But then neither were Berino's innuendos of avarice and deceit. Those had got my back up. I'd begun Hermandad hoping to spare others the miseries I had gone through, and now here I was being treated as just another charlatan jumping into the adoption business for the money.

I also couldn't help feeling that we had been misled a bit by

Francisco Lacuna. He had given me the impression that my visit to the Philippines was to be simply a helpful formality. He hadn't told me that we would need the ministry's prior approval before submitting applications, and he sure as hell hadn't prepared me for Berino's hostility.

I was also rankled by the question of fees. Of all the objections raised by the ministry, the one most offensive to me was the suggestion that our fees were exorbitant. I probably had not helped our cause by showing all our costs, both domestic and foreign right up front. But even so, $7,500 was not a high price to pay for an international adoption in 1986. So I suspected that the ministry's objection probably had less to do with the total figure than it did with how we arrived at that figure.

Whatever the explanation, the result of all this was to plant some seed of doubt in my mind about Paco's effectiveness. My immediate concern, however, was to get my letter into the ministry's hands as quickly as possible. I had two reasons to hurry. One was simple impatience with bureaucratic delays. The other was more personal. Of the four files I had left on Berino's desk, one belonged to two young people I particularly hoped to help.

Dick and Ann Partridge had come to Hermandad after having been turned down by a number of more established agencies on the grounds that they were too young and too insecure financially to undertake the responsibilities of adopting a child. My first instinct on meeting them had been to disqualify them for the same reasons, but by the end of our first interview I sensed enough strength and good sense in this determined couple from rural Connecticut to change my mind. I agreed to take them on, and during the months in which I shepherded them through their home study and preliminary paperwork, I had grown to like and respect them both enormously. Dick and Ann Partridge had been very much on my mind when I was sitting in Luisa Berino's office.

*   *   *

When I wrote my letter to Ina Sanchez, the Philippines was in chaos. Aquino had won the election held on February 7, 1986. Marcos' refusal to accept the results of the balloting had thrown the country into what was, by local standards, a relatively bloodless revolution. The army had gone over to Aquino. Marcos and his wife had been spirited out of the country in a U.S. Air Force aircraft, Corazon Aquino had declared herself the head of the new revolutionary government, and every public functionary in the country was, as Paco wrote me, left sitting *"on tenterhooks for the moment with the apprehension of being reassigned."*

Paco was still in Manila when the revolutionary government came to power. Phone service to that city had been so disrupted, however, that I wasn't able to get through to him. So on February 22, I drove up to Boston and mailed my letter to him with instructions that he deliver it to Ina Sanchez or her successor at the ministry. I also threw in a huge box of chocolates for Paco Lacuna's cousin.

Paco wrote me back on March 12, acknowledging receipt of the chocolates *("It took me three days to wade through customs red tape before I could claim the package")* but making no mention of what he had done with my letter. He expressed *"surprise to know about the letter written to you by Mrs. I. Sanchez,"* but advised that, *"there is no real cause to be unduly alarmed for the battle has not yet begun."* Mrs. Sanchez was a *"political hack"* who would soon be replaced by the revolutionary government. He was sure that other firings would follow. *"I think,"* he speculated, *"that these changes of personnel will benefit us, although it is too early to tell."*

I don't doubt that Berino was one of the first *funcionarios* who Paco hoped would get the axe.

8

Everything seemed on track

WHILE I waited to see what impression my letter would make on the new administration at the Ministry of Health, I again called Alex Sanders. He was jubilant about the Aquino victory. He reminded me of his earlier prediction and reiterated his belief that no one I had met at the ministry would remain in office once the new government got itself organized. I told him about my letter from Sanchez. "I'm not surprised," Alex said. "Luisa Berino is probably in bed with a couple of big American agencies, and your application for approval just means extra work for her. If I were you, I'd just start all over again with the new minister."

I wasn't quite ready to write off all my previous efforts. I told Alex I wasn't going to make any decisions before talking again with Paco Lacuna.

"Didn't I tell you that guy's your problem!" he laughed. "Anybody with that name isn't going to get to first base with Corey's government!"

A couple of days later I got a call from Alex's wife, Lilly. Lilly Sanders sounded as timid as Alex was cocksure. She apologized for imposing herself on a stranger but said that her husband had been telling her about Hermandad and that she just wanted to call to say how much she admired what I was doing. She confessed that while she herself had grown up in comfortable circumstances in Manila, even her family's affluence had not insulated her from the poverty all around her. Her own dream was to do something for her native city's homeless children, but she only dreamed.

I told her quite truthfully that so far I hadn't been able to do much of anything.

Lilly wondered if she could help. She said she had a close friend who was involved with the Benito Aquino Memorial Foundation and through whom she could reach the ear of Corey Aquino herself. But the main thing was, she didn't want to be a bother. If I would rather that she not pull strings, I should just say so.

I suggested that we meet. Lilly said she would like that very much. So Sandy and I drove over to her house, and we spent an afternoon batting around the possibility of some kind of joint endeavor in the Philippines. Alex came by to join us. He was a fidgety, intense man with a goatee who spoke bluntly and seemed to identify personally with the underdog. Sandy disliked him right away.

I pegged him as one of those sixties types, both cynical and altruistic, who put "Question Authority" stickers on their bumpers and saw everywhere conspiracies by those in power to screw the little guy. But I had to admit that I liked what he seemed to stand for better than I liked the man himself.

Sandy was just as uneasy about Lilly. "Right from the get-go," she said later, "there was something about that woman that for me didn't quite add up. For one thing, she'd never look you in the eye. And there was something else too. She'd put out all this stuff about her family's wealth and connections, and here she was working as a clerk in a grocery store! I mean, somehow Lilly Sanders didn't look or act like she'd been brought up with a silver spoon in her mouth!"

But I accepted Lilly for what she said she was. I could think no ill of anyone who wanted to help children, and whatever mixed signals I picked up from her I attributed simply to cultural differences. My strongest recollection of that meeting and of the several that followed was of Alex's rudeness to his own wife.

Alex's cavalier attitude just made me more anxious to help poor, mortified Lilly turn her dreams into reality. Trying to cheer her up after one of Alex's put-downs, I suggested that she write a brief outline explaining how she would go about helping Manila's poor. I told her of my recently established foundation and acknowledged that hers was the kind of effort I'd like to support.

The next time we met, Lilly hesitantly handed me her proposal to begin a program she called Helping Hand, Inc., which would provide food, shelter, and clothing to needy street people. It would set up medical clinics, offer free immunizations, foster cottage industries in impoverished communities, and take other measures to empower the poor. Lilly would serve as executive director. Her staff would be made up of volunteers drawn from her many friends in Manila.

Alex suggested that Helping Hand could undertake at no cost the same services to Hermandad that Francisco Lacuna had agreed to furnish for a fee. His wife's proposed organization could assist in identifying adoptable children, monitor all documents while applications were being processed, keep prospective parents informed about their application's progress, and serve as hosts to those parents if they chose to visit the Philippines.

At the time I thought—naively to be sure—that her plan was reasonable. My only objection was to the substantial salary for the executive director shown in the budget. I had heard Lilly speak often enough of her own family's wealth and position to believe she really didn't need an additional income, and I reminded her that she might have better luck recruiting volunteers if, she, too, worked for no salary. Lilly agreed that she would have ample reward just from "helping children to have a better future," and reallocated what had been her salary to "equipment and overhead." I came up with the idea of assessing all of Hermandad's clients adopting a Philippine child a $200 fee that would be donated to Helping Hand, in the same way that I asked my clients who adopted Guatemalan children to help support Juanita's school. I thought that these contributions would encourage adoptive parents to retain some link with their new child's homeland.

Lilly incorporated all of my suggestions into her proposal and resubmitted it with a request for $40,000 to cover the first year's operating costs. This amount was a lot larger than my tiny foundation could afford, so I helped her draft an abbreviated version requesting $10,000 with the program "to be reevaluated in four months for further assistance."

A few days later, Lilly called me to report excitedly that she had talked unofficially with some of her own friends at the Ministry of Health, who had "pre-cleared" her proposed program and were waiting expectantly for her arrival in Manila. Her other good news was that these same friends confirmed that both Berino and Sanchez had been fired.

I was delighted. I hadn't received any reply from the ministry to my letter. Paco didn't seem to be doing much of anything. Lilly, on the other hand, was champing at the bit to go to the Philippines and willing to stay there for however long it took to set up her own project and get Hermandad properly accredited. So on May 29, 1986, I wrote Francisco Lacuna informing him of the new arrangement and that I was terminating our contract. Paco accepted this news gracefully.

The only thing now delaying Lilly's departure was money. The Sanderses had filed for tax-exempt status for their new organization, but, given the amount of time the IRS normally took to act on these applications, I was afraid another couple of months might be lost before my foundation could act on Lilly's proposal. My solution was to offer her a personal loan of $10,000, with the understanding made in writing that the money was to be repaid *"when Helping Hand is recognized as a nonprofit charity under the United States IRS regulations, but, in any event, no later than December 31, 1986."*

Lilly left for Manila in July, carrying a letter from me authorizing her to act on behalf of Hermandad in the Philippines. An acquaintance of hers named Nancy Ingalls traveled with her. Nancy Ingalls was active in a number of charities and she also wrote for the local newspapers. Alex and Lilly had persuaded her to do an article on Helping Hand, with the understanding that the organization would underwrite her travel costs and that while in Manila she would stay with Lilly's parents.

On the day of their departure, Lilly and Nancy Ingalls arrived at

Boston's Logan international airport, where Lilly discovered with horror that she had somehow managed to leave Nancy's ticket at home. Nancy Ingalls had to pay her own way. The flight to Manila was uneventful, but once there, Nancy got another surprise. Lilly went off to call her mother, and returned with a long face to report that her parents were entertaining house guests and that the two of them would have to stay the night at a hotel. So they took a taxi to the Manila Hilton. Lilly's embarrassment at this awkward change of plan was so great that as soon as the taxi drew up in front of the hotel, she rushed into the lobby to make their reservations, leaving Nancy to pay the fare. Then at the check-in desk, Lilly made a show of further horror at the discovery that she'd also left all her credit cards at home. Nancy paid for their room.

During the days that followed, Nancy's nightmare continued. After moving from the hotel to a squalid neighborhood where Lilly found them accommodations, then being taken to visit a depressing orphanage in the company of apparently uncaring officials, and finally having her own credit cards stolen, Nancy's patience finally ran out. She demanded that Lilly get her on the next flight home. Effecting hurt feelings, Lilly dumped her off at the airport, where she found herself abandoned with neither money nor credit card. She was rescued by American Express and flew home. Too embarrassed about the incident to tell even her friends about how she'd been conned, she was later to suffer further embarrassment when it became known that Lilly had listed her in Helping Hand's articles of incorporation as the organization's vice president.

I knew nothing of any of this and only learned of Nancy's sad story much later. I waited impatiently for news from Lilly and finally did get a letter from her, dated August 18. This was the first written correspondence from my new partner that had not been first vetted by Alex, and I discovered that the woman I had appointed as my representative in the Philippines was not as literate as one would have surmised from reading her earlier proposals.

"Dearest Mrs. Birdsey," wrote Lilly in a childish scrawl, *"I'm sorry I'm so busy trying to set-up everything here in Angeles. I have an endorsement*

for our projects. Amazingly enough everything went well. The people here are very accommodating. They are still looking for younger children to adopt as the kids in orphanages are already bigger than the ones you requested. I'm trying hard to see if there are kids available in the area. We'll talk to you soon. They asked for a big donation. Love, Lilly."

The endorsement Lilly spoke of came from the head of the Ministry of Health, Dr. Cristina Martes, who stated in a letter that *"The ministry approves of the Helping Hand proposal which includes soup kitchen and food bank components. We approve of raising funds for the project in the United States and elsewhere. . . ."* She concluded by saying, *"We feel that this project complements our present policies in the welfare home and adoption sections of the ministry."*

While glad to learn about the endorsement, I knew, from what I had seen myself in Manila, that there were indeed young children in the orphanages, and I suspected the ministry was stonewalling. This prompted me to fire off another ill-considered broadside, this time to Martes, in which I questioned the accuracy of the information her agency was giving out, and thus its integrity, and regretted that the new administration was no easier to work with than the last.

Admittedly it was not very wise for me to send this letter. But I frankly couldn't face another long, drawn-out dance with another incompetent bureaucracy. I wanted to do adoptions in the Philippines. The children were beautiful, and I'd seen many who weren't even held when they were being fed. My impression was that even if the physical care provided to Philippine children was adequate, the loving care so selflessly given by even the most impoverished foster mothers in Guatemala was sadly lacking. I guess I was upset at the bureaucrats responsible for overseeing so heartless a system.

Alex phoned me on September 15 to report that his wife had important news and that I should call her as soon as possible. I waited until it was evening in Manila, and when my call finally went through, I found myself talking to a very upset Lilly.

Her story went something like this: After receiving Martes' program endorsement, she requested an interview with the official in charge of intercountry adoptions and, upon being shown into that official's office, had found the person behind the desk to be none other than the infamous Luisa Berino, who had somehow survived the Aquino purge. Berino had not been cooperative. But Lilly had found a way to out-smart this nemesis. She had learned of an orphanage far away from Manila in Lucena that had more children than it could properly care for. At some effort, she had twice traveled to that orphanage and had been assured by the official in charge that it was possible to arrange direct adoptions by having the natural parents surrender their child through the local Ministry of Health office. Lilly assured me that this procedure was not only perfectly legal but also a great deal faster than going through Manila. Unfortunately, it did involve some additional expenses. My clients (Lilly was carrying the Partridge's application) would have to come up with another $3,000 for legal fees and child care. They would also have to complete some additional paperwork, and it might be necessary for them to travel to the Philippines to pick up their child. If they were willing to do these things, a healthy infant boy named Mario was immediately available. To prevent Mario from being snatched up by some other agency, Lilly urged me to wire her $1,500 as quickly as possible.

I relayed all this to Dick and Ann Partridge, along with as much of a description of Mario as I was able to give. We discussed the risks of pro-ceeding on the basis of such sketchy information but, in the end, put our faith in Lilly and decided to go ahead. I wired Lilly the money, and she sent me the required forms. The Partridges filled these out, and I mailed them back. Helping Hand assumed temporary custody of Mario. Everything seemed on track.

Lilly returned to Providence late in September. The Partridges drove over and we all spent an evening with the Sanders looking at slides of Lilly's trip to Lucena, talking about Philippine culture, and admiring pictures of little Mario. Dick and Ann were ecstatic. So was I.

On October 15, I met again with the Sanderses. Alex increasingly seemed to be taking the lead in orchestrating events in his wife's organ-ization. He said he was about to leave for Manila on business of his own and suggested to me that while there he could buy a car that Helping Hand could use to transport Hermandad's clients from Manila to

Lucena. As he explained it, the alternative to driving was a long and dangerous bus trip, which would be another source of stress to parents arriving to pick up their children.

That made sense. But Helping Hand still had not received its non-profit determination from the IRS. So I wrote out a check from Hermandad's account, pointedly making it out to Lilly instead of Alex. This one was for $5,000 to buy a car.

When Alex returned from Manila later that month, he reported that President Aquino had appointed a prominent attorney named José Morales to head a task force charged with overhauling the country's adoption procedures. He said he had used his connections to obtain an audience with Morales, and the latter had warned him that Hermandad's provisional license still presented an obstacle to its operating in the Philippines.

I called friends at the Office for Children and, with their help, managed to expedite processing our application for a regular license. The license was issued on November 25. Everything now appeared to be a go for the Partridges. The Ministry of Health had forwarded us Mario's birth certificate, his parental surrender papers, and certification that the child was then in the custody of Helping Hand. The U.S. Immigration and Naturalization Service had cleared the child to enter the country.

Alex, off again to Manila, offered to save the Partridges the cost of airfare by bringing home their son for them. Dick and Ann, already in over their heads financially, agreed to this, and on November 27 Alex flew to the Philippines carrying Hermandad's license, the Partridges' written authorization to act on their behalf, and their second $1,500 installment, which was to cover legal and child-care fees.

A month of growing tension followed. I heard nothing directly from Alex. My frequent phone calls to Lilly were always met with the assurance that her husband was meeting regularly with José Morales and had the situation under control. Told this same tale once too often, I finally lost patience and asked Lilly if a complaint to the Philippine Embassy in Washington might help to light a fire under the ministry. Lilly thought that was a fine idea. So I called Scotty's wife, Nancy, in

Baltimore, and Nancy drove to Washington to plead Hermandad's case at the Philippine Embassy.

On December 13, 1986, Alex Sanders returned from the Philippines without Mario. The Partridges were devastated. I was furious.

Alex's explanation was as follows: Upon his arrival in Manila, he learned from Morales that there had been a change in regulations and no adoption done outside the main health office in Manila would any longer be permitted. Alex demanded an interview with the minister herself and received her assurance that as soon as Morales's task force reviewed Mario's case to insure that everything was in order, she personally would sign off on the adoption. He went back to see Morales, who guaranteed him that Mario's would be the first of nine similar cases of children "caught in the middle" that he would review. Morales anticipated no problems, but, in view of Hermandad's previous difficulties with the ministry in Manila, he suggested to Alex that matters might move faster if Mario's case were taken over by an agency already doing business in the Philippines. He mentioned a well-known Boston-based agency as a possible alternative.

Thus it seemed that all I could really fault Alex for was his failure to pass along this information soon enough to spare the Partridges the days they had spent nursing the false hope of having their new son home with them for Christmas. I was impressed by Alex's apparent access to people in high places but puzzled by Morales' suggestion that the Partridges find themselves another agency. Hadn't all the issues concerning Hermandad's qualifications already been settled? Alex said they had not. When he met with Martes, she raised virtually all the same reservations about Hermandad as had her predecessor, Ina Sanchez. He specifically asked Martes if she had seen my reply to Sanchez's original letter. She said that she had not, nor was there any record of my letter having been received at the ministry. Alex could only surmise that Lacuna had never delivered my letter. Martes had accepted a copy of Hermandad's permanent license, but Alex's impression remained that until the ministry's other objections were answered, we were not likely to be approved. He urged that I consider Morales' suggestion that we find another agency to handle the Partridges' case.

I didn't like that idea at all. I knew from having been asked to do the same thing myself that any other agency we approached to take over an adoption in progress would infer correctly enough that they were being asked to take on somebody else's problems. Besides, the Partridges were by now almost like family to me, and I wanted to be the one to get Dick and Ann their child. So I gritted my teeth and wrote a shorter, more temperate letter to Martes, repeating the points I had made in my letter of almost 12 months before to Ina Sanchez and once again requesting that Hermandad be approved by the Ministry of Health.

I might have saved myself the time. My letter, mailed on December 15, crossed one of the 19th to me from the ministry, which alluded to Alex Sanders' visit but stated that no "new working relationships" were being considered.

I didn't know which way to turn. On the one hand Alex Sanders was telling me that Martes was going to sign off on the Partridges' application as soon as it was reviewed by Morales' task force. On the other, Martes' letter advised me that Hermandad's application for approval was, for the moment at least, dead. So where did all this leave poor Dick and Ann? I decided I'd better start preparing them for the worst and told this to Alex.

He urged me not to alarm the Partridges unnecessarily. His advice was to let the task force review the case and then see what happened. Against my better judgment, I agreed.

January dragged by without any action by the task force on Mario's case. In February I met again with Dick and Ann, who, for the first time since we had started working together, seemed uneasy in my presence. Dick admitted somewhat sheepishly that they had talked with the Sanderses and that Alex had advised them to get another agency. That hurt, but I said if that's what they wanted, I'd help them find one.

I called the agency Morales had earlier suggested. Lauren Speed, the social worker from that agency in charge of Philippine adoptions, happened to be leaving the next day for Manila, and she agreed to see if she could find out why Mario's case was moving so slowly.

I drove over again to tell this to Dick and Ann personally. They proudly showed me Mario's room and all the other preparations they had made for his arrival. I found it very sad. By this time I was beginning to doubt Alex's continued assurances that all was well, and I tried, as gently as I was able, to remind this young couple that a lot could still go wrong. They wouldn't listen. Their faith was now in Alex, and he had convinced them that he would get them their child.

Alex and Lilly traveled together to Manila on February 26, 1987. Before they left, they also visited the Partridges. According to Alex's later deposition, Dick and Ann were concerned about whether the people taking care of Mario had enough money. They offered, without being asked, to help out with an additional $2,000. Alex, and Lilly gratefully accepted.

Alex neglected to mention in his account a fact the Partridges later confirmed. On accepting the $2,000 in cash he claimed Dick and Ann forced upon him, Alex had warned them not to tell me of this transaction. When they asked him why they shouldn't, he intimated that my heavy-handed meddling was the reason Mario was still stuck in Lucena and that, if he was to get things back on track, the less I knew the better.

Lauren Speed returned from Manila in early March and called me to report on what she'd found out. "As soon as I mentioned Mario's name," she began, "every head in Berino's office snapped around. Berino told me she'd advised Lilly Sanders months ago, and in no uncertain terms either, that there was absolutely no chance in the world of that case ever being approved."

"Months ago?" I gasped.

"That's what she said!"

I sat a long time too stunned to move before picking up the telephone again to make one of the hardest calls of my life. I dialed the Partridges' number, reached Ann, and repeated word for word Lauren Speed's report from Manila. Ann took the news like the trooper that she was. "It's even worse than you know, Barbara," she said quietly. "Before they left for Manila, the Sanderses asked us for $2,000 more, and we gave it to them. They warned us not to tell you we'd done it."

I promised to drive to their home the next day to see how we could pick up the pieces. I didn't have the heart to go alone. Sandy and I drove together, and I told Dick and Ann in person that in all likelihood they would not be getting Mario for a son. I also left them a check for the $2,000 the Sanderses had taken from them.

On March 12, 1987, as president of Hermandad's Board of Directors, Scotty wrote Lilly Sanders advising her of Hermandad's decision to sever all relations with Helping Hand, effective immediately.

In a second letter of the same date to Berino, Scotty conceded that while Hermandad had believed *"Mario was offered through a legally acceptable procedure,"* it now appeared that *"we may not have been in possession of all the facts and that we have inadvertently caused a problem within the ministry."* He stated Hermandad's "full intention to do whatever is necessary to clear up this situation," including *"withdrawing our application for recognition if that is the wish of the ministry,"* but he added that he hoped that there might remain some way the Partridges could *"still be considered as potential adoptive parents for Mario."*

The ministry wrote him back expressing regret "that we cannot approve the placement of Mario to the Partridges."

*   *   *

Dick's and Ann's ordeal should have ended there. But the Sanderses weren't done with them yet. On April 13, the same day the Partridges learned from us that no further hope of getting Mario remained, Alex Sanders telephoned them to suggest that if Ann would go with Lilly to the Philippines, somehow they would manage to get Mario out. He followed that call with a letter explaining how he *"tryed* [sic] *for four months at my own expense. . . to get the situation squared away but Barbara kept going over everyone's head causing problems for me and Mario. . . So here we are today taking the blame for the whole problem, with no one ever being concerned about Mario's welfare or ours and the ongoing expenses we continue to incur. . . Lilly and I are very hurt and upset by these turn of events and will continue to be positive because we are not quitters. Plus we will not let self-serving people destroy what we have worked hard for."*

Dick and Ann advised the Sanderses by letter that they did not want any further contact with them in connection with their efforts to adopt a Philippine child.

*   *   *

More evidence of the Sanders' chicanery came to light in the civil suit I brought against them. Among the letters Helping Hand's attorney turned over to the court was one from Martes dated August 27, 1986. Sent via Lilly to me, it stated that the ministry was rejecting the adoption application of the Partridges and was returning the application. Lilly had chosen not to forward this letter on to me. Then, on January 9, 1987, Berino wrote to Lilly confirming *"once again that we do not approve arranged adoptions since the ministry has the sole responsibility to match/select a child to foreign prospective adoptive parents."* These letters make it obvious that Alex and Lilly must have known by January of 1987 at the latest that Mario would never be legally released to the Partridges.

This is probably why Alex was suddenly so insistent in urging me to transfer the case to another agency. By the end of 1986, both Alex and Lilly must have been feeling increasingly out on a limb. Berino was pressuring Helping Hand (in letters that also came to light during the pre-trial investigation) to reveal the whereabouts of Mario, and Alex, who knew that physical possession of the child was his trump card, was stalling frantically. Getting the Partridges' case transferred from Hermandad to another agency must have seemed to him his best hope of still cashing in on the couples' longing for that particular child. I wonder if the idea of changing agencies came originally from him or, as he claimed, from Morales. It seems likely that not all of the many meetings Alex and Lilly reported having with influential officials actually occurred.

The organization's financial records were equally condemning. Helping Hand's "home care center," whose sole resident was little Mario, turned out to be staffed by Lilly's mother and father along with three other of her relatives. Significant sums of money allegedly spent on "residents" actually went to providing restaurant dinners and dental care to the "staff." Other operations also existed primarily on paper. Helping Hand made some small but well-publicized donations to the medical care of indigents via a populist newspaper, but otherwise did little else to accomplish its stated goals.

The record showed that one hundred dollars was paid to Mario's mother, thus raising the possibility that the child had been bought and paid for. Nobody knows what became of the automobile intended to carry adoptive parents to Lucena.

*   *   *

Looking back on it now, I have to admit I was taken for a ride by two pretty amateur con artists. As Sandy spotted right off, Lilly was plainly not truthful about her background. Her deceits, her arrogance, and her clumsiness were all the rather pathetic mannerisms of woman with little education who had grown up in the shadow of wealth and suddenly found herself in a position of undreamed of influence. Alex can only be described as literate in comparison with his wife. His own correspondence, which consists largely of fulsomely written paeans of self-praise, reads like a parody of bureaucratic jargon. Comparing his "official" communications (letters to Martes and the like) with the letters he wrote alone suggests that he must have received editorial help from someone. The original proposal, for example, was well typed and contained no misspellings. His letter to the Partridges, by contrast, would hardly have earned a passing mark in a fifth-grade English class.

So how could I have been taken in by a pair of such transparent frauds? I think I might have been quicker to recognize Alex and Lilly for what they were if the events I've recorded here hadn't been played out against the backdrop of Dick and Ann Partridge's longing for a child. For this young couple, Mario was their baby. They had spent a happy evening with me looking at his pictures. They had spent countless hours and a lot more money than they could afford doing everything asked of them to bring him home. They had even bought his crib. They were desperate, and in a sense so was I. My determination to unite the Partridges with little Mario and to make a success of my agency led me to do exactly what I always warned my clients against doing. Intent on my dreams, I ignored the obvious.

*   *   *

My civil suit against the Sanderses was eventually settled out of court. Alex and Lilly agreed to admit for the record that they had known before accepting the Partridges' $2,000 that the adoption they were promising to arrange was no longer possible. They further agreed to repay one quarter of the money they had dunned from Hermandad, the Partridges, and me. Because there had been no contracts stipulating the specific services expected of the Sanderses for monies received, my attorney felt it unlikely we could recover a greater amount if the case went to trial. As part of the settlement, I agreed to seek no further damages.

9

Is there no way to do right in this business?

"YOU know what still bugs me about Alex Sanders?" asked Sandy one day after the smoke had cleared. "Whenever I get something in the mail from organizations who claim to be saving whales or feeding children or helping Indians or whatever, now I smell a rat. Funny thing is that son of a bitch has made me into a worthy-cause junky. I read every damned appeal cover to cover! I mean, there I am eating my breakfast and instead of feeling bad because cattle ranchers are chopping down the rain forest or whatever, I'm wondering if these people, who want money so they can do something about all these horrible problems are for real. And that really bothers me. They probably are good people, and they probably are doing what they say they're doing, but I still can't help suspecting it's all just another scam. That man has made me gun shy! I just don't trust non-profits anymore."

I too had become gun shy. I was still faced with the problem of having more clients than available children, and I still had to investigate other sources of referrals. I contacted public officials in Chile, Mexico, and in India, but in each case obstacles, real or imagined, led me to back off. I found myself suspecting everyone I talked to, and, because I valued trust, I hated myself for it. Worse yet, I no longer trusted my own judgment. I'd always believed that most human beings were basically decent and that the best way to be treated fairly oneself was to treat others fairly. I didn't think of myself as naive. I'd been burnt before, but it had never particularly bothered me. I'd always thought it better to trust others and run the risk of being let down, rather than to go through life always looking over my shoulder.

The Sanderses had hit hard at this sunny view of the world. Alex and Lilly weren't just friends who had broken some small promise or business people who had reneged on a deal. These were people who had cynically played with a child's future and a young couple's dreams. I had known that evil existed. But nothing in my life to that point had prepared me for meeting it firsthand.

I wasn't sure any more that I was the right person to be running an adoption agency. I had always worn my own feelings on my sleeve. When I was trying to adopt a child of my own, I'd been put off by what had seemed to me the hard-nosed attitudes of many of the agency people I'd run into. I wanted my own agency to be more human. After having spent too many years being shunted around between emotionless bureaucrats, I wanted to become involved on a personal level with the families that came to me in search of a child.

Now, with the experience in the Philippines still rankling, I had to face up to the fact that I would need more than good intentions to hold my own in a business that was just as cut throat as any other. If I was to make Hermandad a success, I saw myself being forced into the same cynical, suspicious, hard-nosed mold I so resented. I wasn't sure I could do it. I knew I didn't want to do it.

Another sad turn of events followed the Philippines disaster. Earlier in the year, at a time when I was still pinning my hopes on the Sanderses, Juanita had called from San Félix with both good and bad news. The bad news was that popular sentiment in Guatemala was increasingly turning against the idea of international adoptions. The good news, if you could call it that, was that she had been approached by an Indian girl, eight months pregnant with her fourth child, who was in such poor health that she was terrified she might lose her baby before it was baptized. She'd asked Juanita for a loan to see a doctor and for help finding a home for the child she knew she could not raise herself.

I'd wired off money enough for the girl's medical bills and then, pre-occupied with the growing Philippine crisis, almost forgotten all about that incident until Juanita called again a month later. I was in my office and feeling awful when the phone rang. I'd just returned from telling Dick and Ann about Alex's scam and was completely bummed out. But when I heard Juanita's voice on the other end of the line, I'd remembered the Indian girl and felt a surge of hope. Here perhaps was a child for the Partridges.

But that, too, was not to be. The Indian girl had walked down from the mountains to tell Juanita that her child had been born dead. She'd brought with her what little money she had to repay the money I'd sent her and promised the rest as soon as she was able to raise it. Juanita had not accepted the money, and the poor girl had gone off, filled with shame at having failed to deliver the child that she'd felt was her part of the bargain.

I put down the phone near tears. Dear God, I thought, is there no way to do right in this business? I felt like a wounded animal. I wanted to crawl back to my cave. I wanted to get away from sordidness and misery. And I also wanted to strangle Alex and Lilly, whose own cheap intrigues stood in such stark contrast with the instinctive decency of that poor Indian girl.

Scotty urged me to stay the course. "You went into this with your eyes open," he reminded me. "Even if you just help *one* child, Barbara, it's still worth the effort."

"I've got that one child, Scotty" I told him bitterly. "Her name's Tamsin, and because of Hermandad she's growing up without a mother."

We agreed that we would take on no new clients. We had 13 families already signed on. I'd do what I could for those 13. After that, I'd see how I felt. Scotty agreed to fly with me one last time to Guatemala to see what we could accomplish.

That is how I found myself on that May evening of 1987 on a plane with Thin Tie, the radical priest, the drunken Americans, and my mercurial partner, who, a few days later at a remote mountain orphanage, was also to concede that our dream was dead.

* * *

Hermandad went inactive, but I still felt a responsibility to our former clients. All of the potential sources for children I contacted talked of long waiting lists and extensive delays. Then late in July an old colleague of mine from the Department of Public Welfare sent me a copy of a letter written to the department by the director of a Ohio-based adoption agency called Children and Families (CAF), which had children immediately available for adoption. CAF described itself as an agency that placed children all over the United States. Its board of directors and staff, said the letter, were *"Christians who attend the Church of Christ,"* but CAF worked *"with all faiths—people who can provide warm, stable homes for children."* Attached to the letter was an information sheet listing one Honduran boy, age 18 months, and two *"brown haired, light complexion girls,"* both age seven, all available *"immediately."* Other Honduran children, described only as *"over age three,"* were also said to be available for immediate assignment, as were *"U.S. black infants, bi-racials and sibling groups."* Parents pursuing a Honduran adoption *"must travel. Singles may apply. Usually two short trips. Five days first trip, and three–five days second trip."*

I checked out Children and Families with our Office for Children in Boston and was told that no one there had heard anything unfavorable about that agency. Sandy called the Ohio Department of Health and Human Services to see if CAF was properly licensed. The department confirmed that it was. She then called CAF's director, Sarah Hagen, who provided a straightforward and professional description of its operations and procedures.

Sandy had been impressed enough to describe some of our more difficult cases to Mrs. Hagen as potential clients. Two she mentioned by name were the Partridges and also Laverne Hopkins, an unmarried librarian who was having problems because of prejudice in some countries against single parents. Sarah was clear on the Partridges' particular situation and felt very positive that CAF would be able to find them a child. Regarding Laverne Hopkins, Sarah told Sandy she would charge her $1,000 less than usual and was confident they would find just the right child for her. Sarah also assured Sandy that she felt there were many babies without families yet.

I called Sarah Hagen myself and also got the impression that CAF, Inc. was a thoroughly professional outfit. Mrs. Hagen again stated that her agency had never yet failed to complete an adoption for its clients and urged that "time was of the essence" if she was to act for the Partridges and Ms. Hopkins. She said she and her husband, James, were leaving for Honduras the following week and would carry these two applications down with them if I could get the necessary paperwork and fees to them on time.

CAF sounded good, but I didn't want to risk getting Dick's and Ann's hopes up again until I knew more about the organization. So I decided to mention this possibility instead to the Warberg-Joneses, an older couple who I thought would be better able to evaluate the uncertainties and face disappointment if things didn't work out. I also thought Laverne Hopkins was enough of a realist to assess the odds for herself.

Both Ms. Hopkins and the Warberg-Joneses agreed to proceed. We mailed off fees and forms in time for Sarah and James Hagen to take everything to Honduras. Sarah Hagen confirmed receipt of $7,000 in a letter dated August 12 and enclosed photocopies of two checks, totalling $884.50, that she had "already had to write to cover costs of authentication and expressing the documents in order to be able to take them with us."

After my experience with the Sanderses, I liked that kind of efficient, straightforward accounting of expenditures. Everything else I learned during many telephone conversations with Sarah while she was in Honduras only served to increase my confidence in CAF. Sarah reported that she had seen the child who would be assigned to the Warberg-Joneses and that the boy "sure was cute" and also "healthy as a hog." Laverne Hopkins' prospective daughter was to be brought into town the following day so that Sarah could confirm that that child also was healthy.

Sarah always rattled on enthusiastically about the latest in an apparently limitless supply of adoptable children she had managed to locate during her trip. CAF's stable of immediately available offerings grew from phone call to phone call until it included a three-year-old boy, a six-year-old girl, a set of triplets, a four-month-old boy, and a pair of infant twins. My doubts dispelled, I set about matching up these candidates with my remaining clients.

The Partridges jumped at the chance to get twins. An older couple, George and Wendy Fuller, opted for the three-year-old, and another family, the Falstaffs, set their hearts on the four-month-old boy.

Sarah and James Hagen returned home to Columbus late in August. I spoke to them there by phone on the 24th and followed up this call with a letter of the same date to say that I'd just talked again to the Partridges, *"who don't quite dare to believe there may be infant twins in their future."* I stressed *"how much we at this agency have come to care about this very loving couple,"* and closed with *"many thank you's for your concern in helping to unite children with these parents who so very much desire a family."*

Sarah wrote back promptly, saying *"Go ahead and send the documents for the Fullers and the Falstaffs. We have the children available. Also, the $3,500 for each will need to be sent as the cost of processing the documents is very expensive. Time is of the essence so this will need to be done as soon as possible. The Partridges' $3,500 will need to be sent also, but before it is we will verify the assignment of the twins."*

On August 28, Sarah wrote again. *"We have assignment of the twins for the Partridges. You can go ahead and send their documents to the consulate. Also please send $3,500 for processing fees as the consul expects to be paid as soon as he gets the documents. The total fees for the twins will be $7,500. Oh, by the way we still have a one- and two-year old girl sibling group and a two- and three-year-old boy and girl sibling group. If you have any families that would be interested. They sure are cute."*

A hand-written note from Mrs. Hagen's secretary on the margin of that letter advised that, rather than wait for the Partridges' retainer, CAF had already mailed it's own check on their behalf to the Honduran consulate. I liked that. If CAF was willing to front its own money, I was certainly willing to overlook Sarah Hagen' annoyingly frequent reminders that "speed was of the essence" in sending along the fees!

*   *   *

The first clues that Mrs. Hagen might not be the paragon of efficiency we thought her to be came two weeks later. Wendy Fuller called up to ask why she wasn't hearing anything from CAF. The Falstaffs called next. They'd tried repeatedly to get through to Sarah and each time had felt they were being put off. CAF's director was never available. Did I know why?

I said I'd try to find out. Reluctantly, I got back in harness. During those two weeks of relative quiet I had started to relax. Technically, I was out of the loop. I had referred my former clients to another agency, and, when for the first time in many months my phone stopped ringing, I assumed these families were communicating directly with CAF and all was well.

Before I even had the chance to call CAF, I got a concerned call from Rachel Warberg-Jones. "What gives, Barbara?" Rachel demanded. "I called one of the references I got from CAF—a family named Waldron—and they've had their documents in for four months now, and they're *still* waiting for an appointment for their interview in Honduras! If we've got to wait that long, I'd just as soon get my money back and go somewhere else. And while we're on the subject of money, didn't you say we weren't liable for foster care bills until after we made our first trip to Honduras and accepted the child we'd been assigned? We just got a $200 bill for the care of a child we still haven't even agreed to accept!"

"Don't pay it," I advised. "There's been some mistake. You're not responsible for foster care until after your interview."

"I already did pay it," said Rachel. "I don't want that child to starve, even if I don't know his name!"

I telephoned CAF to find out what was going on. It was a friendly call. I was used to nervous clients myself, and, after all, it had only been two weeks since CAF had picked up these cases. I suspected that breakdowns in communication and incorrect billings were simply administrative snafus in a busy agency.

Sarah confirmed that impression. She confided to me, as someone with experience enough to understand the problem, that while CAF's staff in Honduras was good by the standards of that part of the world, Honduras sure as hell wasn't the good ol' U.S. of A.

"Then you'll send the Warberg-Joneses back their $200?" I asked her. She said she would.

"And how about information packets on the kids? I've had calls from the Fullers and the Falstaffs too, asking when they're going to get biographical data and medical histories. They're getting a little nervous."

Sarah agreed to call Bobbie Notaro, her head worker in Tegucigalpa, and tell her to "get right on that."

Then followed a flurry of correspondence from CAF to my four former clients. Sarah and Bobbie Notaro wrote them all friendly letters filled with such sentiments as, "You're just going to *love* this child!" But they gave very little hard information. The Falstaffs withdrew their application and asked CAF for their money back. Whether this was because of unhappiness with CAF or a change of heart, I never found out.

Sandy and I both made a lot more phone calls to Columbus trying to pry loose specific documents for three increasingly nervous families. At one point Sandy was on the phone to Sarah trying to get a medical history for the Fullers' intended child, when it suddenly occurred to her that CAF's director didn't seem to have the slightest idea what she was talking about. "Don't you have an agency form of some kind that sets down the specific information you require?" Sandy asked. "You know, immunization records, childhood diseases, that kind of thing?"

"No," Sarah said, "CAF doesn't have anything like that." She just generally accepted whatever medical records the people in Honduras sent along. Sandy offered to mail CAF a copy of Hermandad's medical history form. "Why don't you do that, Honey?" said Sarah. "That'd be real helpful!" Sandy hung up dumbfounded. By mid-October, I was also beginning to worry. Most of the complaints I was getting suggested no more than inefficiency. But one raised the possibility of outright dishonesty. CAF was continuing to bill my former clients for foster care for their still unknown children. All but the Fullers' child were allegedly receiving private foster care at a rate of $200/month. The Fullers' baby was in a government orphanage, and George and Wendy were billed by CAF's Honduran office for $150 as "a contribution towards the cost of milk for the orphaned children." Wendy Fuller paid the bill and then called the Honduran Department of Health Services to make sure her money was going to the right place. The official she talked to said his department had no policy of assessing any private parties for the support of government-run orphanages. Wendy asked me if she knew where her $150 had actually gone. I passed that question along to Sarah, who promised to "look into it."

On October 19, I wrote CAF's director a long, diplomatic letter reporting that I had tried to contact Bobbie Notaro directly but that she had not returned my call. *"We understand,"* I continued, *"that Bobbie is a very busy woman who has taken a great deal of responsibility for processing these cases. Would it be possible for us to make arrangements through a friend in the Tegucigalpa area to get the pictures and current information about the children including clothing sizes, etc.? We would want Bobbie to know that we are not attempting to infringe upon her job, but simply trying to be helpful in getting needed information for our parents."*

I closed with a list of the specific concerns expressed by three of the four families and followed up with a phone call, this one to James Hagen (because Sarah was sick). I told James I would pay whatever it cost to have Bobbie send all the requested documents and photographs via Federal Express directly from Honduras to CAF. James promised to make sure Bobbie "got right on it," and I then wrote him confirming our understanding.

That was on October 21.

That same day, I undertook to break the logjam James said had developed at the Department of Health Services. I called Juan Betancourt, CAF's attorney in Honduras, who James had told me was handling all our cases except the Fullers, to ask when I could tell the families they could expect their appointments. It was a puzzling phone call. Juan Betancourt had evidently never heard of the Warberg-Joneses or of the Partridges or of Ms. Hopkins.

Worried, I called James back. He was his usual reassuring self. Not to worry, he advised. Attorney Betancourt's English wasn't all that good. He had evidently not been able to understand what I had been talking about.

"Come off it, James!" I exploded. "That guy's English is just as good as mine. Now how about you tell me just what *is* going on here?" James said he really didn't know. CAF used several different attorneys. Maybe he had given me the name of the wrong one. In any event, Sarah would call me to explain everything as soon as she recovered her strength.

Then suddenly CAF changed its tune. Sarah got off her sick bed to fire off an angry letter to me, dated October 22, in answer to what she claimed were my *"daily phone calls regarding our mutual clients for Honduran adoptions."*

"Let me state our original agreement again," she began. *"We agreed to assign children* [to your clients]. *We did indeed assign children and in fact have taken responsibility for their care by placing them in foster homes. As I told you from the beginning, we do not have control over the assignment of social service appointments or how fast the paperwork travels through the government system. It is unrealistic to expect us to do something about a process we have no control over. As you know from your own international work, it's not like going to a fast food restaurant, it does take time and things don't always work out as we expect them to. We expected you of all people to understand this and be supportive and patient. But, frankly, I feel you are encouraging your clients in their apprehension. We will do what we agreed, but you will have to wait just as our clients have had to wait. A natural pregnancy takes nine (9) months to complete. So I would expect you to begin asking and questioning the time delay after that point not after two (2) months as you are doing. Just be patient and give us some room to work."*

Attached to this letter was a fee schedule addressed to "Prospective International Adoptive Parents," which showed significantly higher rates than the ones Sarah had originally quoted to Sandy over the phone.

This letter took me by surprise. I had spent enough hours on the phone with Sarah and James to think of them as pretty good people. Both had a kind of down-home charm that I enjoyed. Both seemed to be trying their best, and for that one virtue I was prepared to forgive their many apparent inefficiencies. The revised picture I had drawn in my mind of this couple was one of good-hearted fumblers who, for all their apparent ineptitude, really were, as they always signed their letters, "For the Children." Even Wendy Fuller's missing $150 hadn't shaken my faith in what I still believed was the Hagen's essential honesty. Following that incident, I had suggested to them as a friend that they might do well to take a closer look at their Honduran office's bookkeeping procedures. But even those procedures seemed to me more lax than dishonest. Nothing in my relations with Sarah and James led me to expect this sudden chill in our relationship.

I showed the letter to Sandy, suggesting that probably Sarah was just sick and overworked.

"Maybe," said Sandy, "but I doubt it. I'm beginning to notice that that lady seems to have a habit of getting sick on Fridays."

"You think maybe James wrote it for her? He did seem a little bent out of shape when I confronted him with the Juan Betancourt screw-up."

"James?" she laughed. "I don't know. All I know is he really pissed me off! I mean, I like the guy, but I don't get the impression he's playing with a full deck! Every time I talk to him he's got something screwed up. Like those information sheets we sent him. Here I go and do *his* work for him by writing up a long questionnaire with everything on it CAF ought to be finding out about the kids they're assigning, and what happens? I call him to see if he's got the goddamn things, and he tells me he thinks Sarah sent them down to Bobbie. So I ask him if she sent them Federal Express like we asked, and he says he isn't sure. Then I remind him that we got a lot of worried clients who've paid him a lot of money and who really want the answers to the questions on those fact sheets *soon*, and he says, sure, he understands how they feel, and Sarah'll get right on it if she hasn't already. I mean, yuck! What the hell does it *take* to light a fire under those people?"

Then it hit me. "Not again!" I whispered. "God Almighty! Have I let the same thing happen all over again?"

"You okay, Barb?" asked a worried Sandy. "You look like you've just seen a ghost!"

"Yeah, I'm okay," I smiled weakly. "I'm just considering a whole lot of 'what-ifs.' What if we've been suckered again, Sandy? What if all this 'aw shucks' crap and all this getting passed back and forth between Sarah and James is just a good act by two good cons? Because that's the way it's beginning to look to me."

Sandy nodded slowly. "To me too. But Jesus, Barb! What else could we have done? We checked them out every way we knew how, and they passed with flying colors. I mean, if Ohio Human Services gives CAF a clean bill of health, how the hell were we to know?"

"We couldn't. At least, I guess we couldn't. Where I blew it was to allow our families to pay out all that money up front before getting some form of written contract from CAF . All we really have are your notes from that first talk you had with Sarah."

Sandy nodded slowly.

"Goddamnit, Sandy!" I choked. "How am I ever going to break this to Dick and Ann?"

"Maybe you won't have to, Barb. Let's not jump to conclusions."

"No," I said brokenly. "I know it's not going to work. Once you factor intentional deception into the equation, everything else that's happened falls right into place. Those guys are cons. They're giving us the run-around, and a lot of people are going to get their hearts broken all over again, and it's all my own damned fault!"

"Horseshit!" exploded my old friend. "Pardon my French, Barb, but that's just plain crap! You're always taking everything on your own shoulders. Legally, Hermandad doesn't even come into the picture. Our *former* clients are big boys and girls. It's their money and their deal. If they'd wanted a contract when they shelled out the bucks, they could have asked for one."

True, I guess. But that's not how I did business. I had gotten people who trusted me into this mess. Now I would have to get them out of it.

10

If I ever decide to be a crook

*J*ANSWERED Sarah's letter on October 27, 1987, listing all of the broken promises CAF had made to my former clients and pointing out that *"considering the amount of money they have advanced for these assignments, it is little wonder that they would want some information about the childrens' whereabouts and legal status, not to mention conditions of health."*

I made no apologies for my daily phone calls. *"Since we referred* [these families] *to your agency,"* I said, *"we* will *assist them in getting their questions answered."* I was equally firm on the subject of CAF's revised price list, advising Sarah that we would expect her to *"honor the arrangements you made with our families and not expect them to be subject to this amended fee schedule."*

Sarah never answered my letter.

The Partridges were the first to crack. Having heard nothing from anyone since their twins were allegedly assigned to them, they had tried repeatedly to reach Bobbie Notaro in Honduras. Bobbie never returned their calls, and when finally they did get through to her, she announced nonchalantly that "these things take time." Ann begged her for some news of the twins but learned only that they were still somewhere "up in the mountains." It was all too much. Dick called me and asked that I withdraw their application. I wrote Sarah again, asking for *"a full return of monies forwarded* [by the Partridges] *to CAF,"* includ-ing *"the cost of translating and authenticating their documents, as these never would have been sent in the first place without the guarantee of the assignment of the twins to them."*

Then the Fullers' patience ran out. They called Sarah demanding to know who in Honduras was supposed to be making their appointment with the Department of Health Services. Sarah gave them the name of an attorney, whom they then called. The attorney assured them that their case was being processed at the Department of Health Services and gave them the name of the official with whom they were going to meet. George Fuller called him. "Fuller?" said this puzzled official. "We have no application for anyone named Fuller. Who is Fuller?" George and Wendy decided then and there to catch the next plane down to Honduras to find out for themselves what was going on.

I again called the Ohio Department of Health and Human Services to see if anyone else was having similar troubles with CAF. I reached a Sally Martin in the Division of Child Welfare, who told me that there was in fact some concern in the licensing unit about CAF's overly opti-mistic recruiting. CAF was being asked to "tone down" their brochures.

I asked if there had been any specific complaints from clients. Martin said she'd heard some talk about a woman who'd recently called from somewhere in the South to say that she had been paying CAF's foster care bills for several months but had yet to receive any informa-tion about the child she was supporting. I told her I knew a lot of peo-ple who were having precisely the same problem. But I made it clear that I was speaking off the record and did not want to register a formal complaint against Sarah and James Hagen, for fear of jeopardizing whatever chances remained for my former clients to complete their adoptions.

Sally Martin was sympathetic. I assumed my call would be kept confidential. Evidently it was not. Sarah got word of it and launched into such a tirade about my "complaining to the state" that I saw no choice but to request that the Ohio Department of Health and Human Services step in as a mediator between me, as agent for my former clients, and CAF. I listed the specific questions I wanted addressed:

First, what were the Hagen' qualifications for running an adoption agency?

Second, why was CAF's Honduran contact, Bobbie Notaro, failing to release specific information about children allegedly already assigned to clients?

Third, what happened to the money paid to CAF by its clients? Was it kept in individual escrow accounts, and if so why would not CAF provide an accounting when requested?

Fourth, what was the agency's real time-frame for completing an adoption?

Fifth, why was Sarah Hagen virtually impossible to reach during normal working hours?

Sally Martin said she would take these questions to her supervisor and promised to get back to me as soon as she had anything to report.

Meanwhile, I was fielding increasingly panicked calls from my former clients. Ann Partridge reported tearfully that CAF was refusing to refund her $3,500. She and Dick had found another agency, this one dealing with Russian orphans, but until they got their money back from CAF, they couldn't afford to pay the up-front money this agency required. I gave them $3,500, with the understanding that they would pay me back if and when CAF returned their money.

Laverne Hopkins, no less worried than the others, told me she still saw no alternative but to stick with CAF. As an older single woman, she realized she stood little chance of being accepted by another agency. Fearful of rocking the boat, she limited her complaints to pathetic appeals that CAF at the very least send her a photograph of the child she had been promised.

The Warberg-Joneses had no inhibitions about raising a fuss. Rachel, in particular, had little patience with incompetence, and in her eyes James and Sarah were simply the greatest pair of fools she had ever met. She didn't suspect them of dishonesty, only of ineptitude, and she felt she could bulldog them into doing what plainly they were incapable of doing on their own. So she laid it all out for them. She demanded the name of the person providing her promised son's foster care. She asked that this person call the boy "Ramón" so that he would get used to hearing the name she and her husband had given him. She made it plain that she would henceforth require of CAF twice-monthly progress reports on how Ramón was doing and also receipts for all expenditures made on his behalf. She accepted Sarah's explanations for the continuing delays in getting her appointment scheduled with the official agency but insisted that CAF would have to absorb any additional foster care costs if her case went on beyond six months.

Sarah replied to this list of demands with a curt letter advising the Warberg-Joneses that the mother of their intended child had changed her mind and decided not to put the boy up for adoption after all. Rachel's and Bob's composure finally cracked. They spent several days in dumb shock at the loss of little Ramón before getting themselves back in hand and rationally assessing their alternatives. They were familiar enough by now with the international adoption business to understand the risks. They saw no better alternative than to accept Sarah's offer to find them another child.

The Fullers were already on their way to Honduras.

Under pressure from the Ohio Department of Health and Human Services, CAF in mid-November finally released to me an accounting of expenditures paid from fees received. I went over these receipts with a fine-tooth comb, and what I found further fueled my suspicion that Sarah and James were being dishonest. In a letter to Sarah dated November 24, I specifically refuted the legitimacy of $8,400 of expenses for travel, phone bills, and credit card charges and questioned various others as well.

Before my letter got to Columbus, I received a threatening epistle from an attorney, Sam Goldstein, representing CAF and demanding that I "...*cease and desist all objectionable activities engaged in by you with respect to the adoptions being handled by CAF and all communications with the Ohio Division of Child Welfare which could unjustly damage CAF in any way whatsoever.*" The letter concluded with the notice that, "...*if you fail to cease the above activity and if your actions thereby unjustly damage CAF, I will have no alternative but to aggressively safeguard the interests of my client in accordance with the remedies available at law.*"

Four days later I got a furious reply from Sarah to my letter of the 24th. No more *"Dear Barbara,"* this time. *"Dear Ms. Birdsey,"* she wrote, *"let me state my position with you* briefly:

(1) You asked for an explanation of monies spent. I sent you one. All payments are in regard to Hopkins, Warberg-Jones, and Fuller. Until I had these three clients, I had much less expense.

(2) I know now not to give you details as to who people are because I can't trust you to act like a professional. You have violated rules of professionalism seriously and constantly.

(3) These clients—Hopkins, Warberg-Jones, Fuller—need to be contacting us directly. . . .We will not work through you.

(4) Juan Betancourt told you he had not heard of these cases because he did not know you and you are not a client. He does not give out details to strangers. You had no business *contacting him in the first place.*

(5) Have the Warberg-Joneses contact us if they have any questions, etc. We would be happy to tell them what we know. Have them contact us directly *if they plan on continuing.*

(6) In regard to the Partridges, we feel we did as we agreed. May we again suggest it was client failure due to a lack of patience?

We can't win with you. You are always looking for something wrong."

I read this pack of lies, reread attorney Goldstein's letter, and concluded that I was the one who couldn't win. Even if Goldstein was just blowing smoke, I knew enough about law to suspect that Hermandad's corporate identity wouldn't provide me much protection if I were found by some court personally liable for "unjustly" damaging CAF I had nightmare visions of Sarah and James in the witness box; two simple middle Americans wiping away tears as they described how this uppity eastern woman's meddling had thwarted them in the work the Lord had called on them to do. I'd been taken in by Sarah's downhome charm. No doubt a jury could be also. I asked myself what right I had to risk my own family's financial future for the sake of this quixotic crusade? None, I concluded. The stakes were too high.

But could I just walk away from this mess? I'd already reimbursed the Partridges for the money they'd lost to CAF. The Fullers had struck out on their own, so my conscience was reasonably clear on their account. But what of Laverne Hopkins and the Warberg-Joneses? Would it be enough if I offered to cover their losses as well?

But what else could I do? Sarah and I were at such loggerheads that probably any further involvement with CAF on my part would just end up hurting rather than helping whatever small chance remained for a happy ending for anyone.

So it seemed that what was best for me would also be best for my former clients. Or so I tried to persuade myself.

"*Dear Parents,*" I wrote the Fullers, the Warberg-Joneses, and Laverne Hopkins. "*We now find ourselves in a difficult position as CAF, Inc. has threatened legal action against us should we continue to have further communication with the Ohio authorities. Sarah Hagen has indicated that she wishes to have direct contact with each family and does not wish Hermandad to be involved. . . . At this point we feel there is nothing more that we can do on your behalf.*"

I sent these letters off with a mixture of regret and relief. Regret because I had not entirely managed to persuade myself that I was doing the right thing. Relief because now at least I could get back to seeing something of my own family.

I need not have written the Warberg-Joneses. Bob and Rachel were having second thoughts about continuing with CAF. Sarah had offered them a choice of three other children, all of them "immediately available," but by then neither one of them felt they could again face the emotional roller-coaster ride CAF had put them through once already. They withdrew their application and demanded a refund of their $3,500, plus the money they had paid for the care of a child they would never see. Sarah refused on the same grounds as she had refused the Partridges. She said it wasn't CAF's fault if they were too impatient to wait for a child.

*   *   *

In early 1988, Sandy and I set about closing up the office. We were stuffing papers into boxes when the phone rang. Sandy answered and handed me the phone. "It's Wendy Fuller calling you from Honduras," she said. "The poor woman sounds nervous as a cat!"

"You there, Barbara?" came a muffled voice from the other end of the line. "I can't talk any louder because I don't want Bobbie to hear me. I'm at her house now. My husband had to go home, and I've been staying with the Notaro's for two weeks alone, and I don't dare leave because if I do I'll never ever get to see my kid. But I'm scared to death. I sit here at night and listen to Bobbie telling lies to would-be parents all over the United States!"

"What kind of lies has she been telling?"

"You know Ramón? That little boy CAF supposedly assigned to Rachel and Bob? Ramón's just a photograph! The boy whose picture they sent was never really a candidate for adoption. Same thing with Laverne Hopkins' little girl. Somebody's got to stop these people, Barbara! Or else a lot more families are going to get hurt."

I sat silent for a long time, the receiver held tight to my ear. I listened to the cacophony of rapid-fire Spanish that echoed faintly over the long-distance line and thought again of how desperately I wanted to get clear of all this and back to my own children. But I knew how ashamed I would always be if I quit now. There would be time later for my own kids. For reading together and for picnics and for boat trips. Right now everything else in my life would have to take second place to exposing CAF.

"You still there?" Wendy Fuller finally asked.

"Yes," I said, "I'm still here. I heard what you said, Wendy, and I guess that someone is going to have to be me."

*   *   *

The first thing I did was to call the Ohio Attorney General's office, where I was put through to a staff attorney, Nick Fuchs. I told him my story, and he told me that his office could prosecute service organizations such as CAF, if in fact there was reason to believe these organizations were defrauding consumers. He made it sound as if "could" and "would" were two different matters.

"You don't think what I've told you constitutes sufficient reason to believe that Sarah and James Hagen may be defrauding consumers?" I prodded.

"What I am saying is that in a case of this nature, the responsibility for investigation rests with the Department of Health and Human Services as the agency which licensed CAF and which has oversight over its activities. We don't normally get in the act until the department notifies us that there is grounds for civil or criminal complaint."

I told him I'd already spoken to Sally Martin and that their licensing staff had promised to take another look at CAF. But I reminded him that a lot people out there could get hurt while he sat around worrying about who's got jurisdiction and who's doing what. And I also told him about attorney Goldstein's threat to sue me.

"You willing to risk a libel suit?" he asked.

I hesitated. "Yes," I said finally. "At first I wasn't. Believe me, I'm no hero, Mr. Fuchs. Goldstein almost scared me off. But then I decided somebody's got to stop those people. I know just what those would-be parents Sarah has conned are feeling. I've been there myself. They're hurt and they're ashamed and they just want to crawl into a cave and lick their wounds and forget the whole miserable experience. I expect she counts on those feelings of shame and embarrassment. That's why she can afford to be so brazen. She knows the clients she's screwed aren't likely to come back at her."

The line was silent a long moment, and then it seemed Nick Fuchs reached a decision. "Understand that I'm talking to you now simply as an attorney and not as an employee of the Ohio Attorney General's office," he began. "I like what you're doing, but I've got to tell you to be careful. I'm not trying to scare you. I don't have any inside information on this case, but if CAF really is involved in as big-time a scam as you say they are, they've probably got access to some pretty influential people. So make damn sure nothing you say or write can possibly be used as grounds for Sarah Hagen to claim libel. Keep written records of all your conversations with Ohio officials. And don't ever make any allegations to anyone, even off the record, if you can't back them up."

I said I'd be as careful as I could, but that my best protection was probably that CAF couldn't afford to sue me without putting on the public record a lot of information they wouldn't want in the newspapers.

"Never underestimate your opponent," warned Nick Fuchs. "And don't expect too much from me. If I can't get my boss interested in CAF, I can't do a whole hell of a lot on my own. I'm just a small fry."

I waited a week and then called him again. This time Nick Fuchs did not come out from behind his cloak of bureaucratic caution. He explained there was some question whether or not CAF's alleged negligence constituted a violation of the state's Consumer Protection Act. He had asked for an opinion on this from another attorney who worked with trade complaints, and the two of them were going to meet shortly to review the case.

Sandy called him next. Fuchs said he wouldn't be able to talk to the Attorney General until the end of the month at the earliest. He was pretty busy with other matters. She asked him if he was too busy to hear of the latest allegations against CAF? "No," he laughed, "I'm never too busy to hear more dirt. What've you got?"

"What we've got are photocopies of CAF's checks made out to the attorneys in Honduras who were supposed to be handling our clients' cases. We've talked to these same attorneys, who tell us they've never heard of our clients and never been paid a cent to represent them. All of which makes us think Sarah and James are writing checks but never sending them to the payee shown. That way they can document spending our clients' money while keeping it all for themselves."

"Should be easy enough to prove that," said Nick Fuchs. "Aren't there depositors' signatures on the backs?"

"We don't know. Sarah only sent us photocopies of the fronts. What makes us suspicious is that none of the checks show any of the kinds of stamps and whatnot you generally see on *both* sides of cancelled checks."

"Send them along," said Nick Fuchs wearily. "I'll add them to the file."

"They're already in the mail!" said Sandy. "By the time we're done sending you stuff, you're going to need more than a file on CAF. You're going to need a goddamn warehouse!"

*　　*　　*

Nick Fuchs called on April 11, 1988 to report apologetically that Ohio's attorney general had decided not to take the case, citing three reasons: first, because none of the people complaining were Ohio residents; second, because a civil suit would provide a more appropriate remedy than action by the attorney general's office in a case involving financial restitution; and third, because all of the problems we had described were already being addressed as a result of an investigation of CAF just done by the Ohio Department of Health and Human Services.

I asked him if he had seen a copy of the department's investigation. Nick Fuchs said he had not. So I wrote Health and Human Services asking for a copy of their investigation. In reply, I got a letter dated April 25 from the assistant director, Marshall Costa. Costa thanked me *"for the information you provided us in regard to your dealings with Children and Families (CAF), a licensed adoption agency in Columbus, Ohio. . . . As a result of the concerns you and others expressed, the Ohio Division of Child Welfare of the Department of Health and Human Services conducted an investigation of the agency, its practices and administration, and its compliance with licensing rules. Several noncompliance issues were discovered relating to qualifications of staff and record keeping. Under our supervision, CAF has corrected the deficient areas. We believe this will result in a better administration and program for the agency and its clientele. We will be closely monitoring CAF during the next year to assure continued compliance with licensing rules and appropriate agency practices."*

"If I ever decide to be a crook," said Sandy, "you can bet your ass Ohio's the place I'm going to go to be one!"

11

A different kind of Christmas present

"She told me not to go!" Laverne Hopkins sobbed into the phone. "*Who* told you not to go?" I asked. I'd been asleep when Laverne called, and between my own fuzzy-headedness and Laverne's incoherent weeping it took a while to get her story sorted out.

Laverne's had been the one case I felt might actually end successfully. The first child CAF assigned her had fallen through. That had been a trauma, but Sarah Hagen had sent a photograph of an alternative, a beautiful little girl, with whom Laverne had promptly fallen in love. From that point on, everything appeared to be going smoothly. CAF made the assignment and put Laverne in touch with several other clients who she understood would also be traveling to Honduras on July 8, 1988, the day before the group was to appear at the Department of Health Services. Laverne and these other families spoke frequently throughout the spring, and when June came without any further details forthcoming from CAF concerning their fast-approaching trip, they had begun to worry, Laverne most of all. She was the only single mother in the group. She rarely traveled anywhere outside Massachusetts, and the prospect of flying to Honduras with a group she knew only from phone conversations filled her with terror. Nonetheless, she bought her ticket. On July 6, she called Sarah, who gave her the name of the woman she was told would meet her in Tegucigalpa. Then, to make doubly sure there would be no hitch, Laverne called this woman direct on the 7th.

The woman had never heard of Laverne Hopkins and had no plans to meet anyone of that name at the airport the following day. Laverne by then knew enough of CAF's chronic poor communication with its Honduran agents that she was not overly surprised. She gave the woman the name of Cora Martínez, the attorney assigned to represent her at the Department of Health Services, and asked that her now-alerted guide call Martínez to get things straightened out. Then she went to bed. An hour later her phone rang. It was a collect call from her Honduran attorney. "Don't come tomorrow," said Cora Martínez. "We have no child here for you."

That was when Laverne called me. As I listened to her telling me of her latest nightmare, I had an idea. It was a long shot but worth a try. I asked her if she'd be okay by herself for an hour or so and promised to call her back.

Laverne said she'd be okay.

Then I called George Roberts, a political counselor in the American Embassy in Mexico City, whose wife, Jessica, had been a college friend. By coincidence, Jessica Roberts had telephoned me just the week before to report that she and George had adopted a little Mexican boy. I had laughingly asked her if she intended to start an army. The Roberts had six other children.

My call caught George in the middle of dinner. "George, I've got an emergency," I said by way of excuse for interrupting his supper. "I need the name and phone number of the woman Jessica told me was so helpful arranging your latest son's adoption."

"Right now?" asked George Roberts.

"Yes! Right now! Someday when I've got more time I'll tell you why. Okay?"

"Okay. Her name's Bertha something. Wait a sec. I'll ask Sue." A minute later he was back with the information I needed.

Bertha Ponson was also eating dinner. I explained who I was and what I needed. It seems my call was providential. Bertha was just then trying to find another home for a little orphaned girl she herself had become very attached to. She had placed this girl with a Mexican family, but there were problems with that family's other children, and they had returned her to the orphanage. Bertha asked me to send her the necessary documents by Federal Express. If everything was in order, she didn't see any reason why Laverne Hopkins couldn't make the first of the two trips necessary to complete the adoption as early as August.

I called Laverne back. "Can you wait until August?" I asked.

"For what?" Laverne stammered. She was still barely able to speak.

"To meet your Mexican daughter!"

"*Mexican?*"

By the time I finished explaining it all to her, she was no longer sobbing.

*   *   *

Wendy Fuller, meanwhile, had come back from Honduras with her assignment in hand. Awaiting on her return was a bill from CAF for the second installment of $3,500. This she refused to pay. The terms of her original understanding with Sarah Hagen, as relayed through me, were that this second installment was not due until her child was actually in the United States with all the necessary paperwork complete. Moreover, she had done virtually all of the work in getting the appointment with the Department of Health Services. CAF's sole contribution had been to locate an adoptable child, and for that Wendy figured she had already paid quite enough. She said as much to Sarah Hagen. Sarah replied that either the Fullers pay up or else she would use her Honduran connections to stop the adoption. Panicked at that possibility, Wendy sent her the money.

Incensed that the state of Ohio wasn't going to do anything about CAF, I was determined not to let the matter rest. When looking for ideas in a scrapbook I kept of newspaper clippings on adoption-related issues, I rediscovered an article from a Connecticut paper headlined "Adoption Case Leaves Legacy of Disappointment." It told of a case the Connecticut attorney general had brought against my old friend, Sue Hampson.

Sue's luck had at last run out. After her Honduran attorney absconded with her clients' funds, the clients had come after Sue for their money. She argued that it was not her responsibility to pay back money someone else had stolen. Her clients then took the case to Connecticut's consumer protection unit, and there the case was referred to a hard-charging assistant attorney general named Mike Anderson. Anderson's investigation uncovered all kinds of irregularities in Sue's way of doing business. He threw the book at her. She lost the case, repaid the money, and moved to Arizona.

Persuaded that this was just the sort of attack dog I wanted to sic on CAF, I called Anderson's office and was put right through to him. Anderson hadn't forgotten Sue Hampson. "She was a piece of work, that one!" he laughed.

"Sue might have bent the rules a bit," I agreed, "but maybe that's what it took to get as many orphaned children as she did out of Central America."

Anderson said his job was not to make the laws, just to prosecute the people who didn't follow them.

"Well then," I laughed, "have I got the case for you!" I went on to tell Mike Anderson everything I knew about CAF, including the fact that two of CAF's clients—Warburg-Jones and the Partridges—were my former clients and lived in Connecticut.

He was interested. But he warned me that he couldn't do anything unless his boss let him take the case, and even then the best he could hope to do would be to recover my former clients' money and perhaps get an injunction barring CAF from doing further business in Connecticut. He couldn't stop them from doing business anywhere else. This wouldn't help repay Laverne Hopkins and the Fullers, since they were Massachusetts residents, but we had to start somewhere.

Anderson's boss did let him take the case. I passed on everything about CAF I could get my hands on, and Anderson pursued the leads I gave him with the same single-mindedness he had brought to the Sue Hampson case. He interviewed all of CAF's Connecticut clients (the Warburg-Jones put him in touch with two others), talked to his counterparts in Ohio, and, in November 1988, flew out to Columbus to obtain affidavits from all the principals at CAF. He was wonderful, efficient, and caring.

Laverne Hopkins' case, meanwhile, was moving through the Mexican welfare system. Her appointment to pick up her child was scheduled for December, and as the date drew nearer, Laverne grew increasingly apprehensive. The shock of losing the second child she'd thought she'd been assigned by CAF had affected her deeply. She had suffered chest pains severe enough that she was been hospitalized with a suspected heart attack. Her pains were ultimately attributed to anxiety. Three months later, she remained very much on edge.

I decided to go with her to Mexico City. Sandy, Laverne, Tamsin, and I flew down two weeks before Christmas and were met at the airport by an obviously harassed George Roberts. The entire American diplomatic staff was getting ready for the inauguration of the new Mexican president. George had been assigned to the reception committee for President Duarte of El Salvador and said apologetically that about all the help he could offer was to put us up at his house and lend me a car.

That car turned out to be an almost windowless van without rear view mirrors. For the next five days—sometimes with Bertha as a guide, sometimes on our own—the four of us and however many of the Roberts children were at loose ends made the rounds of orphanages and ministries. Laverne's new daughter, Mariposa, was allowed by the nuns who had charge of her to come with us. She, Tamsin, and the Roberts children hit it right off, and the back of the van became a riotous playpen. I did the driving. Bertha's last-minute directions to "take the next right" usually found me in the passing lane on Mexico City's crowded freeways, and my blind dashes across traffic in that mirrorless van didn't endear me to Mexican motorists or do much for poor Laverne's peace of mind.

We could never find a place to park. For two consecutive days I spent four hours in that van full of screaming children circling endlessly around the square in front of the ministry where Laverne and Sandy were trying to get little Mariposa's amended birth certificate. The policeman at the ministry gate found the sight of my continuous orbiting a huge joke. Every time I would try to pull into a place in front of the building where I could have parked without bothering anyone, he waved me off, grinning broadly, and then waited for me to come around again to repeat the same performance. I could have strangled him.

Late on the second day of this ordeal, a Friday, Sandy flagged me down to report that the official in charge of issuing passports had decided to go home early and would not be able to complete processing Mariposa's application until the following Monday. I was near the end of my rope. "Here, Sandy, you drive this goddamn mobile nursery!" I demanded. "Let me go in and talk to that guy!"

"No way I'll drive that thing!" Sandy wailed. I had to move. That bastard policeman was waiving me on. "Okay then," I hollered as I pulled away, "you'll have to do it yourself. But don't come back out of that building without Mariposa's passport! You do and we're going to miss our flight on Monday."

Sandy and Laverne were both back outside in time to intercept me on the next orbit. "Did you get it?" I demanded as they climbed into the van.

"No," Sandy admitted, "but we did get the name of a regional office that's open Saturday mornings. The guy told us if we drove out there, they'd finish up processing the application tomorrow."

That night at dinner, George Roberts firmly vetoed our plans to drive out to this other office. "It's too risky," he said. "It's a long trip and a dangerous place. You'll just have to reschedule your flight and wait until Monday."

I was just as adamant that we had to go. Poor George, who was sick with the flu, decided that if I was going to be that pigheaded, he'd have to go with us. So early the next morning, we drove for an hour far out into the suburbs. We weren't early enough. By the time we arrived at the ministry office, the line of passport applicants already stretched right around the block. George used his diplomatic status to go to the head of the line. We got the passport but had to sneak out the back door to avoid being lynched by the furious mob, who wasn't at all happy about rank-pulling gringos.

On Monday morning we went to the U.S. Embassy to get Mariposa's visa. There we learned that the Immigration and Naturalization Service in Boston had failed to send down Laverne's file. I had anticipated that and brought with me duplicates of all the necessary forms. Then it developed that the only official who knew how to process visa applications was sick. So I and a very junior foreign-service officer sat down with the visa "how to" manual and issued Mariposa a preliminary visa.

Even then, we weren't out of the woods. Regulations aimed at controlling the exodus of Mexican workers into the United States required that all Mexican nationals present their visas at specified border crossings. We were told little Mariposa would have to report to the U.S. consulate at Ciudad Juárez, just across the border from El Paso. George called ahead to see if he could again get us to the head of the line, but it didn't work. The U.S. official at Cuidad Juarez refused to give us preferential treatment, and we ended up spending two days standing in a line of literally hundreds of Mexicans who were waiting for work permits.

It was a long two days, made more bearable by the good humor of the Mexicans with whom we waited. It was only with their help that we were even able to eat lunch and go to the bathroom. When finally late on Wednesday we did reach the head of the line, we were searched before being allowed inside the consulate. Sandy, footsore and angry, refused to give up her camera.

This scene was interrupted by a loud-speaker announcement that it was closing time. So I made a scene of my own that was impressive enough that cowed officials fell all over themselves stamping Mariposa's visa.

We started across the border, were detained midway for two more hours by U.S. Immigrations, and when Laverne Hopkins' new daughter finally stepped for the first time on American soil, it was ten o'clock that night.

*   *   *

My Christmas present was waiting for me when I got home. A grinning David handed me a clipping from the *Hartford Courant* that was headlined "Adoption Agency Sued, Attorney General Claims Fraud."

The civil action brought by the State of Connecticut against Sarah and James Hagen, individually, in their capacities as president and vice president respectively of CAF sought *"orders enjoining* [the defendants] *from misrepresenting the availability of possible adoptive children and the progress of adoptions; from failing to deliver adoptive services; from failing to honor their own refund policies; and other unfair and deceptive acts and practices in the offering of adoptive services."* Connecticut also asked for *"full monetary restitution"* to injured consumers as well as $30,000 in civil penalties.

The case was heard on April 5, 1989. Neither Sarah or James appeared in person. They were represented by a Columbus attorney, Charles Gooden, who consented on their behalf to an injunction barring CAF from *"offering, delivering or providing any adoption service of whatever description to any person in the State of Connecticut."* The judge also ordered that restitution be made to wronged clients, with the details of payment to be settled between the two attorneys out of court.

Following negotiations that dragged on into the summer, Mike Anderson agreed to waive Connecticut's claim to civil penalties in exchange for which Gooden committed CAF to making full restitution with interest to the Warberg-Joneses, the Partridges, and the other two clients.

Having CAF's attorney agree to restitution and getting CAF to pay it proved to be two different things. Throughout the fall of 1989, Mike Anderson's repeated requests for settlement got nowhere. Sarah Hagen, operating through Gooden, dodged and weaved. Sometimes she claimed lack of funds. Sometimes she promised payment by dates that went unmet. Sometimes she simply didn't do anything.

While all this was going on, I got a call from a Mr. Patrick Flanagan, who directed an Indiana-based adoption agency called Family Sanctuary. He had heard something of my problems with CAF, and, he himself had had unfortunate dealings with Juan Betancourt. He said he was calling me because he had taken the lead among a group of other agency directors to found an organization to be called the "Federation of Adoption Professionals." He wondered if Hermandad would be interested in joining.

I explained that my agency was inactive but that I certainly supported his goals and would be glad to join if his organization accepted individual members. I also offered to submit a summary of my own experiences to the Federation's newsletter.

Patrick Flanagan said he would welcome me as an individual member, but he felt he had to make it clear that both the Federation's newsletter and its computer bulletin board, which he also edited, were intended as vehicles for sharing information and not as forums for airing what might be construed as individual grievances. Nonetheless, I did send him copies of the newspaper articles on the CAF case in Connecticut, with a note that he could do with them whatever he saw fit.

The Federation's September 1989 bulletin board reprinted without comment the *Hartford Courant* article about the state suing CAF. Sarah Hagen replied in the November newsletter: *"In response to the article posted last month, I would like to comment. Our agency was involved over two years ago in a dispute with several clients from Connecticut. These were clients of Juan Betancourt. The children promised by Juan Betancourt did not materialize and this created problems. This dispute with Connecticut has been settled for over one year. Our agency settled with no admission of liability. We were also insured so that no family lost money. We know we have acted responsibly, however this old rumor keeps popping up."* She went on to list some *"lessons learned"* from this unhappy experience and concluded *"Our mission is to help the children. Won't you all please help us do this?"*

When I read that, I almost threw up!

I wrote Flanagan again on November 17, sending him the court records of the CAF case, and pointed out that despite Sarah Hagen's claim to the contrary, *"None of the families involved have received any payment from or on behalf of CAF."* Then I followed up my letter with a phone call to ask Flanagan what he intended to do with the information I had sent him.

Flanagan said he wished I'd never brought the matter up in the first place. "This is exactly what I didn't want to happen," he told me. "None of us who founded the Federation had any intention that our newsletter become an arena for feuding agencies."

I reminded him that he had printed a pack of lies by Sarah Hagen and told him I thought it important that he set the record straight. Flanagan replied that he had no way to know who was telling the truth and no intention to become an arbitrator of disputes. His aim was simply to establish uniform standards of ethical behavior in international adoptions.

I resisted the urge to blow my top and instead asked Mike Anderson to write Flanagan. This he did on February 8th, 1990, requesting *"that a correction be published in the next copy of your newsletter stating that the dispute remains open, and that numerous Connecticut citizens who were injured by CAF's unfair and deceptive practices. . . remain without the reimbursement of the fees to which they are entitled."* Anderson sent copies of his letter to Sarah Hagen and Alan Gooden.

About this same time, Gooden telephoned Anderson to report that Sarah and James had disappeared. Gooden had called CAF's Columbus office and found it closed. He had to advise us that any further efforts to recover money from this now defunct organization would probably be futile. Mike Anderson relayed this information to me and I called CAF in Columbus. A secretary answered. I introduced myself as a prospective client who had been given CAF's name by someone who was not sure if the agency was any longer active. I wondered if CAF was still in the adoption business and, if so, whether the agency had children available. Sure, said the secretary, CAF was very much in business and had any number of children immediately available to clients.

I told this to Mike Anderson. "Rats!" he groaned. Always willing to follow through, Anderson said, "I'll call him right back."

On hearing from Anderson, Gooden expressed relief that his clients were still in Columbus. He allowed as how his mistaken impression that they had left town must have been due to some problem with the phone and promised that he'd get right back on the case and see what could be done. On February 14, he wrote Mike Anderson that *"Money has recently become available to attempt to facilitate a settlement of the financial claims of the three clients. Accordingly, I would appreciate your contacting me at your earliest convenience regarding payment amounts and procedures."* Gooden added a P.S.: *"As an indication of the agency's good faith, we are enclosing a check in the amount of $3,500 as a refund for the agency fee in the Partridge matter."*

That was the only money we were to get from CAF in February.

My April issue of the *Federation*'s newsletter mysteriously never arrived. I borrowed a copy. On the first page, listed prominently among the names of new members of the Federation, was CAF.

Page three of the same issue listed the four *"Most Frequently Heard Complaints from Adoptive Parents."* These included *"(1) Loss of funds ('We paid a large initial down payment and were later told there were NO REFUNDS.'); (2) Dishonesty concerning cost of adoptions ('Family is told adoption will cost $7,000 and it later ends up costing substantially more.'); (3) Inaccessibility of agency personnel ('After the parents pay their money, they find their agency playing hide and seek.'); and (4) Dishonesty about active programs ('Agencies say they have programs in a certain place. After fees are collected, they inform parents program has suddenly closed.').*

"Folks," concluded editor Flanagan, *"we have been getting a great many of these kinds of complaints. I want to add, however, that the agencies mentioned in these complaints (so far) HAVE NOT BEEN Federation members. And, yes, we do hear the same names over and over."*

On the next page, under the heading "WAITING CHILDREN," Flanagan printed the following announcement: *"Sarah Hagen of Children and Families reports she has children waiting for adoption in Mexico, Peru and Honduras. Currently she has one set of four-month-old triplets in Peru (parents need to travel from March 1 to April and stay about four weeks). She also has newborn twins in Peru (six week stay) and newborn twins in Honduras."*

I showed the newsletter to David.

"Looks like CAF's got a monopoly on twins and triplets!" he laughed.

"The hell they do!" I said, annoyed at him for laughing. "Sarah knows that twins sell. Somebody's going to read that advertisement, and they're going to bite, and they're going to be taken to the cleaners! So what in Christ's name could Patrick Flanagan be thinking of?"

*   *   *

Mike Anderson sent copies of his original letter to Patrick Flanagan to the other five members of the Federation's executive board. None answered. The May newsletter contained no mention of CAF's wrong-doings. But despite the Federation's silence, word of the Connecticut action against Sarah and James Hagen was getting around. Mike Anderson's office received so many out-of-state calls from families also seeking redress against CAF that he began referring these calls on to me as someone who had been successful in the same effort.

One person who called me was a would-be single parent named Rebecca Gould, from Minneapolis. Ms. Gould reported that she had applied initially to Patrick Flanagan's agency, Family Sanctuary, and had been referred by Flanagan to CAF, as an agency that had children "immediately available." Since Flanagan had made this referral in March, which was after he had already received notice from Anderson that CAF had been enjoined from practicing in Connecticut, I asked Ms. Gould if he had given her any indication that there had been complaints made against that agency.

"Absolutely not!" she said. "If he had, I wouldn't have done business with them."

Rebecca Gould went on to describe what had followed. She had sent her initial payment of $3,500 to Sarah Hagen and had been "assigned" a Mexican child and put in touch with the other families who would be traveling to Mexico with her. She and her fellow travelers had all been a little surprised when told that they were scheduled to appear in Mexico City during Easter week, but they'd gone ahead anyway and flown down. James Hagen met them there. Nothing in the city was open. They drove with James out to an orphanage to see their children, were met there by nuns who weren't expecting visitors, and learned that this particular orphanage ministered only to physically and mentally disabled children. One by one, they showed the Mother Superior the photographs of their "assigned" sons or daughter. In each case she told them that the child was too seriously retarded to qualify for adoption. The group angrily demanded an explanation from James. He then slipped out a back door and caught the next flight home, leaving his charges stranded in Mexico City.

"Does Patrick Flanagan know all this?" I asked.

"You bet he does!" said Rebecca.

Rebecca Gould's story was the last straw. On May 17, I wrote Patrick Flanagan advising him that *"I cannot remain associated with an organization which, with knowledge of past wrongdoing, would accept an agency such as CAF into its membership and actively help to promote business for them."*

Flanagan was by now beginning to backpeddle. In the aftermath of the Mexican fiasco, Ohio's Department of Health and Human Services was being bombarded with complaints against CAF. A major scandal appeared to be in the making, and his Federation stood likely to be implicated. *"Dear Barbara,"* he wrote, *"I am sorry you have decided to withdraw from the Federation. . . . I plan to reproduce your letter of May 17 in our July newsletter along with other materials I have received on CAF. If you feel strongly enough about CAF, perhaps you would like to attend* [the Federation's Annual Meeting] *and address our membership personally. Again, I am sorry you have decided to withdraw. We need committed people like yourself to make our organization worthwhile."*

I declined this invitation. As I wrote the Federation's board of directors, *"I have supplied ample information about the types of problems encountered by myself and the families I referred to CAF. If further information is required by the Board, I am willing to respond in writing."*

But I began to pester Human Services again with inquiries about why nothing was being done about CAF. On February 13, I'd written the Ohio govenor asking the same question. The governor's office referred my letter back to Human Services, and this led to a letter to me dated April 10 from Louis Jones, the department's director. Jones cited CAF's recent repayment of the Partridges' claim as evidence that the agency was in fact in compliance with the Connecticut court order and further pointed out that, following my complaints in 1987, his Division of Child Welfare had conducted the two-day investigation that led to findings of noncompliance in several areas that CAF had since corrected. *"CAF,"* he concluded *"is currently licensed and in good standing"* with the Division of Child Welfare. Ironically, Jones's letter giving CAF a clean bill of health was written during the same week that James Hagen was shepherding his clients through the orphanage for retarded children in Mexico City.

I wrote Jones again, this time by certified mail, return receipt requested, asking why his division didn't consider the ample evidence that CAF was acting unfairly and deceptively with adoptive parents a violation of its licensing regulations. *"The major problem with officials in Ohio,"* I suggested *"appears to be their failure to look fully into a situation. It is too bad that Connectivut had to do the work that properly belonged to Ohio."*

That last barb must have hit home. *"On the basis of your letter and additional complaints we have received,"* Jones replied on May 23, *"we are beginning another investigation of CAF and are assigning the case to a different investigator."*

The tide seemed at last to be turning.

12

You can't do it alone

"THIS is Marshall Costa from the Ohio Department of Health and Human Services," said the voice on the phone. "Do you remember me?"

I remembered Marshall Costa all too well. "I sure do!" I replied. "Aren't you the one who wrote me two years ago that your division's investigation of CAF had turned up only a couple of administrative problems?"

Costa admitted wryly that was him. I said his mistake had been to assign the same woman to that investigation who had done CAF's original licensing study. He agreed but said this time he was putting two investigators on the case. Their names were Becky Mussina and Joan Warham. He asked me to give them whatever help I could.

I said I'd be glad to and asked in return that he send me a copy of his 1987 investigation of CAF, copies of all complaints filed against CAF, and a copy of Ohio's licensing regulations for adoption agencies. I told him I needed these documents because I intended to write a book about the CAF scandal and wanted to make sure I had my facts straight.

"A *book?*" he exclaimed. "Good Lord! Why? It's not like we're talking big-time crime here!"

I told him I thought CAF's story might serve as a useful warning to prospective adoptive parents who needed to know that they could encounter people like Sarah Hagen and Juan Betancourt in the international adoption business.

He suggested that I was exaggerating the extent of the problem.

I suggested that he was *underestimating* the extent of the problem. "Face it, Mr. Costa," I told him as calmly as I could, "the international adoption business is a natural magnet for con artists. On one end, you've got couples so desperate for a child they're willing to do just about anything to get one, and on the other end, overseas, you've got children that can be bought and sold like commodities. So don't try to convince me that Sarah Hagen is some kind of aberration in an essentially honest business!"

But Costa did try to convince me of exactly that. I found myself remembering his bland assurances that his earlier investigation had solved all CAF's "noncompliance issues," and I lost my temper. "Maybe you just don't *want* to see what's going on out there!" I accused him.

"That's a cheap shot," he fired back. "You people expect government to keep everything safe and healthy and well regulated for you until it comes time to pay your taxes! Then you start hollering for cuts. So then my staff gets cut in half, and I get to be the fall guy when something like this CAF business slips by us. Tell you what, Mrs. Birdsey. Next time you write the governor, you ask him to give me my staff back, and that way I'll be able to do my job right. Okay?"

He had a point. Marshall Costa was decent enough to accept my apology for what had been an uncalled for remark on my part and offered to keep me posted on the progress of his investigation. I asked him what CAF's status was while that investigation was ongoing. He said the agency was innocent until proven guilty. All his office could legally say to inquiries from the public was that there had been complaints against CAF that were being investigated, but that the agency remained legally licensed in the State of Ohio.

All during that summer of 1990 while Costa's investigation was proceeding, CAF continued to advertise nationally for clients. I called Becky Mussina or Joan Warham almost weekly, and each time they told me I'd have to be patient. "Look, Barbara," said Becky finally, "this case is one hell of a mess, and we're trying to get it sorted out, but it takes time. We've got to follow up on each complaint we've received, and we've received a lot of them!"

"I know it must be a nightmare," I agreed, "but what worries me is that all the while you guys are busy investigating past complaints, Sarah's still out there swindling a whole new batch of would-be parents."

"We're going as fast as we can," Becky replied. "We've got two people from our own criminal investigation unit on it, and the attorney general's office has put an assistant on the case. There's also another guy named Monroe from the Columbus district attorney's office who's been asking questions. But it all takes time."

I went back to waiting and to thinking more about this book. The idea of writing up my experiences in the adoption business had surfaced one day when Sandy and I were reminiscing about our times together in San Félix and Manila and Mexico City. "Somebody ought to write a book about all this!" Sandy had laughed.

"I've been seriously considering it," I'd said and realized suddenly that I needed to do it. From that point on, I'd begun trying to be a bit more systematic about keeping notes and records of my correspondence. But the idea had remained a vague one until CAF came along to convince me that somebody needed to sound a warning. I remembered how vulnerable I had felt and how willing I had been to believe anyone who told me what I'd hoped to hear. I thought I might be able to spare others from the same heartbreaks.

By September my ideas for a book were taking firmer shape. I called Marshall Costa and asked if I could interview him and his two investigators face to face. Costa agreed to this, and Sandy and I flew out to Columbus. Our interview began awkwardly. I had no official status, and neither I nor the three Ohio officials felt entirely on firm ground as to what questions could appropriately be asked or answered. I began stiffly by reading from a yellow legal pad my reasons for requesting an interview. I wanted, first, to get some past history on the role of the division in regard to adoptions in Ohio, and most particularly in regard to agencies conducting out-of-country adoptions; second, to learn what I could about CAF's relations with the division; and third, to find out what the division planned to do in the future to prevent deceitful adoption practices.

Items one and two weren't controversial. Costa told me the practice of licensing adoption agencies had begun in Ohio in 1955. The purpose was to protect both children and adoptive parents. There were somewhere between 15 and 20 licensed agencies in the state—he wasn't sure of the exact number. Approximately half handled international adoptions. He used to have five staff in his licensing office. Now he was down to two. He and his staff were responsible for licensing group homes as well as adoption agencies. The minimum educational requirement for heading an adoption agency was a master's degree in a related discipline or an undergraduate degree with three years of job experience. His licensing unit did not normally require criminal record checks on adoption agency employees. The Ohio Department of Health and Human Services was currently investigating two other agencies besides CAF.

Costa wasn't sure when CAF had first applied for a license. It was "probably in 1984." His recollection was that Sarah Hagen might previously have worked through the Church of Christ, although that Church now denied any affiliation with CAF. He thought CAF had been founded originally by Sarah with her former husband, whose name, he believed, was Marco. James had begun as an employee and ended up marrying the boss. The attorney general's office had discovered that Sarah had a criminal record. She'd been charged with passing bad checks, which she'd done under the names of Marco, Senz, and Nicholas, and some others he couldn't remember. She didn't have a college degree of any kind.

I asked him how Sarah had ever been issued a license in the first place. "If I'd known then what I know now, I'd have done a lot of things differently," he admitted ruefully. With that he excused himself to go to the dentist. He never did answer my third question.

Becky Mussina and Joan Warham had said little during all of this. With Costa gone, they loosened up. The four of us walked down the street to a corner grill, and over lunch Becky and Joan talked about their own investigation. They had interviewed angry would-be parents from all over the country. In every case the story had been the same: optimistic promises from CAF, false "assignments," demands for more money than originally agreed to, and finally trips to Honduras to meet children who, if they existed at all, were rarely eligible for adoption.

Becky and Joan had interviewed Sarah and James at CAF's headquarters. Sarah hadn't been able to produce any of the records they asked for. Some she "couldn't find." Others were "confidential." Pictures, allegedly of children placed by CAF, had proven fraudulent. "It was surreal!" said Joan. "Like we were in a Hollywood set for an adoption agency rather than the real thing!" The final straw had come when Becky and Joan broke off for lunch. They'd gone alone to a nearby restaurant where by apparent chance Sarah, James, and several other CAF staffers had also shown up. The two parties had eaten at separate tables and each paid their own checks. Later, when Becky was going over CAF's financial records, she found an entry under the date of their last visit where Sarah had written off the cost of taking two Human Services officials to lunch!

Our own lunch over, Becky and Joan left to go back to work. Sandy and I spent the rest of our day in Columbus with Herman and Betsy Cleaver, a couple from Indiana. Herman and Betsy had been among the families abandoned in Mexico City by James Hagen and were hell-bent on bringing CAF to justice. Betsy had taken it on herself to contact CAF's other wronged clients. The information she obtained, at her own expense in the course of countless hours on the telephone, became one of the cornerstones in the case Ohio was building against Sarah and James. She had heard about me from Rebecca Gould, and we had talked often over the phone. I'd told her I was coming to Columbus, and she had driven over to meet me.

I hit it right off with this feisty little woman. We spent that afternoon trying to top each others' CAF atrocity stories. Betsy had the best one. She told me of a letter she'd received just the month before from Sarah Hagen. Sarah offered her $5,000 if she would drop all claims against CAF and then threatened her with more bills and a libel suit if she didn't accept those terms.

*　　*　　*

As soon as I got home, I called Arthur Young, the Ohio assistant attorney general assigned to the CAF case, to offer my help with his investigation. Young was still gathering complaints from wronged clients, and I agreed to contact every family I knew who had dealt with Sarah Hagen to urge that they forward their stories to Young. I also alerted him to the possibility of a connection between CAF and the Federation.

Arthur Young's investigation, along with those of the Department of Health and Human Services and the Columbus district attorney's office, continued on into the fall. Sarah Hagen carried on as if there wasn't a cloud anywhere on the horizon. Her advertisements with the usual claim of children "immediately available" continued to appear in *USA TODAY*. "That lady is either awful damn dumb or else she knows something we don't!" said Sandy.

I was also beginning to wonder if Sarah and James *did* know something that led them not to worry unduly about the net that seemed to be closing around them. I had not forgotten my conversation with Nick Fuchs of the Ohio attorney general's office, when he'd called to tell me his office had decided not to investigate the charges I had made against CAF. "We're a small office," he'd said at the time, "and right now we're putting all our resources into investigating a suspected fraud in the tanning salon business."

I said, "I can't believe that anyone would think suntans are more important than children!"

So I was worried about Ohio Attorney General's priorities. I wondered if he would see enough votes at stake to give CAF much attention. I also wondered about Marshall Costa's first investigation. That had been a whitewash. Maybe the current investigation would be also. I had every confidence in Becky, Joan, and Arthur. But I was a lot less sure about the men they worked for.

I called Mike Anderson, who was now in private practice, to ask how I, or better yet, somebody who'd been burnt directly by CAF, could go after Sarah privately in the event Ohio failed to act.

"You could get a group together to launch a class-action suit," he suggested. "If that were done in federal court and the plaintiffs won, you'd get a court order against CAF which could be enforced nationwide."

"So why don't we do it?" I asked

Mike could think of a lot of reasons. Cost was one. The difficulty of putting together a case when the plaintiffs were spread all over the country was another. It was also far from certain that there were grounds for bringing the case to federal court, since adoption and consumer fraud were both issues usually regulated on the state level.

I asked him how one would start the process.

"By drafting a letter to every one of CAF's clients whose names you could get your hands on," said Mike. "Ask them if they would be interested in being party to a class-action suit against CAF."

"It shouldn't be hard to get those names," I ventured. "Betsy Cleaver already has quite a list. We could also advertise in the adoption journals. Then maybe once we've got some answers back, we could pro-rate the cost among those interested and see how many would be willing to contribute. What kind of money are we talking about?"

"Probably $1,500 to draft the suit, compile the supporting documents, and present the case in court. If you won, you could probably recover attorney's fees from CAF plus maybe even twice or three times the amount of actual injury you were able to prove Sarah had been responsible for."

I ran an advertisement in three national adoption newsletters asking anyone who'd had *"unsatisfactory dealings with Children and Families."* to *"please send a brief written statement to CAF Concerns. Attention: Mike Anderson,"* at the address of his firm. Twenty-five people answered. The following excerpts from two of their letters are representative. They describe new horror stories and also suggest the complicity of another agency that, as it was never indicted, I've called here Agency X.

One couple from Illinois wrote:

> We attended Agency X's annual potluck supper. Harriet Robin [of Agency X] had placed photographs of children from Mission of

Mercy, Inc. on the wall. Families had to see them as they went through the food line. I felt this was a way to entice us to want the children. It was a way to mentally get you hooked. . . . Harriet told us to take the photo of Joana home with us if we were interested in adopting her. . . . She said we were the first family from her agency to go with CAF.

After several phone calls to CAF, Sarah informed me she was going to Mexico and would look into Joana's case. . . . Upon her return from Mexico Sarah said nothing about Susanna having any problems. She only said that Joana's hair was cut really short. There wasn't any mention that she was in a special needs orphanage.

Later Harriet Robin sent us the requirements for the United States part of the adoption. . . . I asked CAF for the Mexican requirements for adopting their children. After several weeks it arrived after many requests. . . . Harriet helped us [with the Mexican application] because the information from CAF had some poorly written directions. . . . Because of all the trouble we had getting help from CAF, I became somewhat suspicious of their ability to do Mexican adoptions.

I called [a friend] because she was knowledgeable of Mexican adoptions. I told her Joana was in an orphanage run by Mother Theresa of Calcutta, India. She asked me if I knew that was an orphanage specifically for special needs children. I said no and said I was going to call CAF immediately to find out what was going on. . . .

Sarah assured me that Joana was fine. She had been placed there by mistake. . . . We trusted Agency X so we thought CAF's word was trustworthy. We got all our paper work together. . . .

We traveled to Mexico on April 9, 1990. It was Holy Week and the professional people we were to go down to see were out of town on vacation. Then we were told that Joana was brain damaged. . . . On April 12 we were told the orphanage was closed for adoptions. We had no choice but to return to the United States. It was a wasted, expensive and painful experience. I felt I had gone to my daughter's funeral.

I asked Harriet Robin if she thought that maybe James thought more about our contract and money than serving us to get a child. Harriet assured me that of the ten families she had [placed] with CAF, no one would be hurt. James and Sarah Hagen were showing her all their files and she knew all about CAF. . . . Harriet said she would set up an appointment between us, her and CAF to talk over the matter. I told her by law Joana was simply not available for adoption.

The meeting with CAF and Harriet Robin was basically useless. Harriet [sided with CAF] on every complaint we made. She [said] foreign policies were always changing and that is why [our] adoption was not successful. This is not true. Note: Holy Week is *always* observed in Mexico. Joana was *never* adoptable by long-standing Mexican law.

I guess [Harriet wanted me] to be sympathetic towards CAF but I am sorry, my daughter's adoption was at stake along with my $10,000 investment. No way! Harriet knew that CAF was incompetent. . . .

* * *

Another Illinois couple wrote:

Mr. Anderson: Here is our story. It's longer than you might care for, but [we're] too sick of this shit to write another version for every interested party. Good luck and good hunting!

We originally contracted with Agency X to do our home study. Our caseworker was Judy Game [who] told us Agency X had just begun dealings with CAF to arrange adoptions out of Honduras. We had been hesitant to go with a Latin American program because of the need to travel, the threat of international instability, and the vagaries of bribery etiquette. Judy assured us that CAF was very experienced, had a long track record, and top-notch Honduran lawyers who had the process down pat.

A healthy week-old boy was available immediately. Judy suggested we could have our child by June. On March 23, 1990 we signed the contract. We asked Judy specifically if the $11,600 was all the money we were to pay, except for travel expenses. She assured us that it was.

In June, after a confusing couple of months trying to prepare for the adoption, this couple left for Honduras for their appointment with the social-services office.

No one met us [in Tegucigalpa]. We waited 45 minutes, then, as all the taxis were leaving for the day, used our meager knowledge of Spanish and small amount of local currency to get a cab to our hotel. At the front desk we asked about our reservations. They said that we had none. A room was available so we took it and waited for something to happen.

An hour later our lawyer called to ask if we could receive our baby. His son brought the child, a beautiful smiling boy. Upon inspection, we were surprised to find a web of flesh between two of his fingers. . . . The next day our lawyer arrived and told us he had faxed a message to

CAF the previous week telling them not to send us down; he had no appointment at [social services]. He waited until Tuesday to send us with an interpreter . . . simply to beg for a hearing. They adamantly refused us, all but ordering us out the door. When we told them our agency was CAF they grew furious and said CAF had tried to force a couple through without an appointment just the previous month. We left outraged and in tears.

We called James that night to plead with him to pull his many strings. He said our lawyer lied. Our lawyer said he lied. The lawyer asked us for $225/month for foster care. We told him we would make [these] arrangements through CAF. We flew home emotionally devastated, furious at our treatment, and depressed at leaving our son with our case in such a shambles.

We met with Judy to express our growing mistrust of everything CAF told us.Judy said everyone has troubles with international adoptions and indicated that we were overreacting.

We said we had signed the contract with CAF, paid the money to CAF, followed CAF's instructions to the letter, yet CAF took no responsibility for foul-ups. If not them, who should we hold responsible? We hadn't hired the lawyer. We had been told their lawyers were dependable. . . .

*   *   *

While these letters were coming in, Mike Anderson had been looking for the most appropriate federal statutes on which to build a class-action suit against CAF. Two statutes, one dealing with mail fraud and the second with "racketeers and corrupt organizations," seemed to fit the case. He was still concerned about the issue of "numerosity," i.e., whether he would be able to come up with enough plaintiffs for the court to consider the group a "class." Our hope was that more people would come forward as the word spread. In the meantime, Mike wrote letters to the two-dozen-odd parties who had initially expressed an interest in the suit, requesting $200 from each of them to cover the initial costs of bringing the case to court.

Only three were willing to put up money. I was upset. Mike was more realistic. "You can't blame a group who've already been burned before if they smell a rat when I hit them up for more money, especially when I'm telling them I can't guarantee success in recovering either damages or court costs."

I offered to put up the money myself.

"Don't risk it," he advised. "A case like this one really requires the active participation of the plaintiffs. My sense is that these people are whipped. I think they just want to forget about CAF. Drop it, Barbara. I know it's disappointing, but you can't do it alone."

So ended the effort that might have put the case against CAF in federal court.

13

Lookin' for the money

*O*N November 28, 1990, Arthur Young, acting on behalf of the Ohio Attorney General, obtained a temporary restraining order freezing CAF's assets, appointing a temporary receiver for its accounts, and barring the agency from misrepresenting its services. On that same day, the Division of Child Welfare revoked CAF's license. A hearing before Columbus Circuit Judge Anthony Stein was set for December 6.

Becky Mussina sent me a copy of the *Cleveland Plain Dealer* article reporting on these events, as well as a thoughtful letter thanking me for my perseverance. Betsy Cleaver, who had appeared at the court hearing as a witness, called me that evening to report jubilantly how Arthur Young had made mincemeat of the Hagens and their attorney, Charles Gooden. Mike Anderson, who had been following the case, later sent me Judge Stein's court order.

The injunction drafted by Arthur Young and handed down by Judge Stein, was, as Mike Anderson said admiringly of his Ohio counterpart's handiwork, "a remarkable document." Young was sensitive to the problem of applying laws designed to regulating commerce to an issue as emotion-charged as adoptions.

He described how CAF was running essentially a *"bait and switch"* operation in which Sarah and James would assign *"a particular child in a contract, without any certainty that the child was in fact available or would be acceptable, and then offer alternative children once the adoptive parents had already paid a substantial sum, were on the scene in the foreign country, and faced with bitter disappointment if they refused proffered alternatives."* He contended that the defendants, in their roles as *"broker speculators"* in children, had concealed from their clients many important facts, such as their lack of knowledge of the Spanish language and lack of any authentic relations with attorneys or agencies in foreign countries.

And, finally, he produced evidence to show that James and Sarah routinely paid many of their personal expenses out of corporation funds, that they anticipated income *"during 1990 of more than $80,000,"* and that they had recently purchased in their own names real estate in Columbus and Arizona, using more than $50,000 of CAF's money for this purpose.

Gooden, with no real case for the defense, had evidently attempted to shift blame for the malpractices described by the prosecution to the "perfidy" of CAF's foreign contacts. He'd cited "good will gestures" similar to the one made to the Cleaver family ($5,000 to settle and shut up) as evidence of his clients' willingness to do the right thing and, when these tactics failed to impress the court, had resorted on cross-examination to trying to portray the state's witnesses as psychologically too fragile either to hold up to the necessarily arduous process of adopting a child or to be credible in their testimony. He'd been particularly brutal with one single parent, but she'd stood her ground, and this strategy too had backfired.

Young had flown in from all over the country witnesses enough to carry the hearing into a second day. But by the end of the first afternoon the judge had heard enough. He dismissed all further witnesses as unnecessary in making the state's case. A second day of hearings, devoted primarily to hammering out the specifics of the injunction, was held on the 11th, and on Thursday, December 13th, 1990, Judge Stein issued an order granting *"the plaintiff's motion for preliminary injunction and appointment of a receiver."*

The Court did not bar CAF outright from doing further business. Instead it demanded that Sarah and James make disclosures to their clients of a kind that made it highly unlikely anyone in their right mind would have further dealings with CAF. *"Pending trial on the merits"* of the charges brought against them, Judge Stein instructed the defendants that they were not to *"assign"* named children to clients, nor to portray international adoptions as *"quick, easy and simple,"* nor to represent children who might be available for adoption as being in good physical and mental health, nor to falsely represent themselves as having *"custody rights or rights to place children in foreign countries."* Sarah and James were further ordered to inform all existing and future clients that they couldn't speak Spanish, had no contractual relationships with the foreign attorneys, and no guaranteed sources for children. They were not to engage in any financial transactions on behalf of CAF without express permission of the court-appointed receiver. Nor were they to *"sell, transfer, encumber, hypothecate, conceal or otherwise remove"* from the state of Ohio or the state of Arizona any of their own real estate or personal property.

I was jubilant. I called David in from his shop and read him the entire injunction. "Whew!" he grinned. "I guess that'll tie 'em up pretty good!"

"I guess it will!" I agreed, laughing. "Arthur won't even let them 'hypothecate!' I bet they had to look that one up just to find out what it is they aren't allowed to do!"

*   *   *

Mike Anderson wrote to congratulate me on the *"remarkable achievement your efforts have produced."* I knew the credit belonged to Arthur Young and called him up to tell him so. Young seemed less confident about the extent of his victory. "Thanks," he said, "but we really haven't won until we've recovered the clients' money. The state can't actually lay hands on any of CAF's assets until the case comes to trial and the injunction is made permanent. A lot can happen between now and then."

"What for example?" I asked.

"Sarah and James could declare bankruptcy. Then we might end up with so many other claims against their assets that there wouldn't be much left over for their former clients."

As far as I was concerned, the Hagens were permanently out of the adoption business, and, at last, so was I. I'd done what I could. My own former clients and many others would get their money back, and they could start again. Despite Arthur Young's warnings, I was confident that even if Ohio only ended up recovering half of CAF's known assets, that would be ample to reimburse the families who had come forward with complaints against the agency. I was glad Betsy Cleaver had refused to settle for half of what she was owed.

I was eager to get on to other things, but CAF wouldn't go away. Less than a month after Judge Stein issued his injunction, I got a note from Joan Warham enclosing a copy of a letter from Sarah Hagen typed on printed stationery showing a Columbus address, to a Ms. Lucy Wells of Finding New Homes, Inc., in Cairo, Illinois. The letter made clear that while she was no longer operating CAF, she remained very active in the international adoption business as a consultant to families wanting to adopt from Honduras.

Sarah went on to suggest that a particular family (Joan had whited out the name) who had been a former CAF client and was now evidently the client of Finding New Homes would do better to *"allow me to take their case directly to Honduras to be completed."* She would do all the preliminary work and provide Ms. Wells with information sheets on the selected child *"to share as appropriate with the family."* Her letter made no mention of what all this would cost.

"Sometime soon I would like to meet you," Sarah concluded her proposal to Ms. Wells. *"I am only helping several agencies from now on and I would like to work with you. I do this work as a humanitarian gesture and it allows me to study and do consulting work as well. I am deeply interested in Latin American culture. It is my feild [sic] of specialization."*

Ms. Wells had been too clever to bite. Instead she'd forwarded Sarah's letter on to the Ohio Department of Health and Human Services. Joan asked me to pass along any evidence that might come my way suggesting that CAF was still active. Arthur Young made the same request. So I picked up my phone and called a friend in Florida who said she was willing to call the CAF number anonymously to ask about the availability of children.

She decided to use the name Jane Potter and wrote a summary of her call to CAF's old number. "*A man answered. I asked him if this was the CAF Agency. He said no, this is Tony Woods. He* [said] *they* [the phone company] *must have forwarded* [CAF's] *calls to him. He then stated that they* [CAF] *were no longer in business. I asked him why, and he stated that their operating costs were too high. . . . I then stated that I had talked to CAF about a year ago, but that I had been pursuing a private adoption in Florida in the meantime and was getting nowhere. He then stated that he supposes he has sort of taken over where CAF left off. I then asked him what the price would be and stated that CAF had quoted me $10,000. He stated that that was the same with him. I then asked him how much he would need to get started. He stated the full amount. I asked him why. He answered saying that most of the monies goes to the attorneys and agencies in the southern countries, the exact same countries that CAF dealt with, and most of the monies remaining in the U.S. went to the consulates. He says he receives very little for his work. I then asked him if he is dealing with the same countries that CAF* [dealt with], *what their record was as far as acquiring babies for clients. He stated that they had a very good record and that right before they stopped doing business they acquired and delivered a baby in only two months of waiting.*"

At this point Mrs. Potter had grown suspicious. "*I stated that I was not going to simply send him a check for $10,000 and not have some sort of information to look over with my husband first. He agreed and stated that he would immediately send some* [brochures] *out to me. He asked for my telephone number. I gave him* [a fictitious name] *and my office address and telephone number. I tried to leave everything untraceable* [back to me]. . . . *I honestly feel that* [Woods] *is fronting for the CAF organization. . . .*"

So did Arthur Young. He cited Sarah and James for contempt of court. The trial on the contempt petition and on the state's motion to make its injunction against the defendants a permanent one was set for April 17, 1991, again before Judge Stein. Arthur Young did not feel it necessary that I appear as a witness.

On the day of the trial, Young again assembled a representative group of the many injured clients from all over the country. The Hagens, who had since fired Gooden, appeared in court with one of Columbus' better-connected trial lawyers to represent them. Excitement ran high among the assembled witnesses for the defense, all of whom had suffered heartbreak and extensive financial loss at the hands of the Hagens and were now at last gathered to see justice done.

The case of the *State of Ohio, Plaintiff*, vs. *Children and Families et al.* never came to trial. Instead, Judge Stein summoned the attorneys for the prosecution and the defense into his chambers. The outcome of that closed session was a settlement in which the judge dismissed *"with prejudice"* all criminal contempt petitions against the defendants. He permanently enjoined Sarah and James Hagen from *"engaging in the business of providing any adoption services"* in the state of Ohio and ordered them to pay *"the amount of $20,000, for the restitution to victims."*

*　　*　　*

Arthur Young's dismissed witnesses gathered unhappily on the court-house steps to watch a smiling Sarah and James drive off in a car with Arizona plates. "Twenty thousand!" spat one angry woman. "That's not a whole lot more than we shelled out to those S.O.B.'s ourselves! We'd've probably done better to settle for the five thousand Sarah would've paid us to keep our mouths shut." Who could blame them for feeling so let down? What had happened?

*　　*　　*

Now being totally cyncical, I suspected a possible conspiracy. What other explanation could there be for so unexpected and disappointing a settlement? Arthur Young had built a case that seemed unassailable. He'd clearly expected the trial to go forward. Why else would he have flown in his witnesses? He had identified and frozen assets enough to reimburse the agency's swindled clients. Sarah had dug herself in even deeper by earning two contempt citations. I'd even prided myself in thinking that the statement I had gotten from Jane Potter might have provided the evidence that would send Sarah to jail.

Mike Anderson disagreed with my conspiracy theory. "It's precisely because Arthur Young's case *was* so airtight that the case didn't go to trial," he told me. "My guess is that the judge decided not to waste everyone's time hearing evidence when the verdict was already obvious."

"What about the victims, Mike?" I demanded. "Consider just the eight families we know of personally who Sarah swindled. Multiply eight by ten thousand, which I bet is on the low side of what each one of those families was taken for, and you get some idea of the kind of money Sarah and James should have been ordered to return to their victims. So why weren't they made to do it?"

Mike Anderson said I'd have to ask someone in Columbus about that.

*   *   *

The first person I asked was Ernie Johnson. Johnson was one of the investigators from the Ohio Department of Health and Human Services' own criminal investigation unit who had worked closely with Arthur Young on the CAF case. He'd impressed me initially as a bit of a bumpkin, an impression that I later realized he himself cultivated to hide a quick and incisive mind. I'd learned to trust and respect Johnson, and when I called him up I asked him pointblank what had gone wrong in the CAF case. "CAF?" he drawled, "Let's see. Seems to me what happened was when Arthur's people started lookin' for the money, all they could find was $20,000."

I asked him if that meant all CAF's clients are out their money for good. Johnson hesitated before answering. "Well," he finally admitted, "I guess that case isn't rightly closed, but you'd have to say it's sittin' way back on everyone's back burner. I did hear that the postal inspector was snuffin' around some, and Monroe over at the DA's office still has an open file on CAF, but you got to remember that Monroe's also got about 100 homicides to worry about. One hundred homicides already this year, right here in Columbus! Can you believe that?"

I told him I could believe almost anything was possible in Columbus. Johnson laughed. "What I'm sayin' is that when the DA's got 100 homicides on his hands, a white-collar crime, which is how you got to classify the CAF case, is gonna get less priority. I dunno. They might proceed with that case, but my guess is it'll just stay on the back burner."

He'd guessed right. I learned later that the Columbus DA's office had tried to build a case against Sarah and James, concentrating specifically on the events that led to James's abandoning his clients in Mexico City. The effort stalled due to the intransigence of the Mexican authorities, who had not wanted to open that can of worms. The Hagen file was eventually returned to the "back burner," where it remained, open but ignored.

Arthur Young proved unexpectedly reluctant to discuss the case. He did tell me that following the preliminary injunction, he had only been able to recover a small percentage of what he suspected were the Hagen's actual assets. Ohio law had required him to advise Sarah and James 24 hours in advance of his intention to file for a restraining order against them, and by the time the court-appointed receiver had gained access to the Hagen's accounts, $20,000 was all there was to be found. The judge had seen no point in ordering restitution beyond the total of the defendants' assets.

I was skeptical about this version of events. Even given what I saw to be the absurdity of a law requiring advance notice for a restraining order, I wondered how in that short period of time the Hagens could have managed to hide from sight assets that had been estimated at the time of the preliminary injunction to be at least five times more than the amount recovered.

Arthur didn't know. He did say the state had evidence that the defendants had managed to move $15,000 out of reach before the restraining order took effect. He had no idea where the rest of their money had gone.

I asked him why Judge Stein hadn't demanded enough in restitution to repay the victims and given Sarah and James the choice of either coming up with the money or else going to jail on the contempt charges. Arthur waffled a bit on that one. He reminded me somewhat lamely that when the out-of-court settlement had been agreed on, the court had only known of relatively few candidates for restitution. Twenty thousand dollars had seemed a more realistic sum to him, then, before he had received the deluge of additional complaints that reached his office as a result of the publicity the case had received.

I asked him why he couldn't have reopened the original case or else brought a new one against the Hagens based on the testimony of all the families he'd found out about only after the settlement? His answer was that Ohio couldn't try the defendants twice for the same crime.

"So what *can* Ohio do?" I demanded.

The fairest thing, said Arthur wearily, was to do what he'd already done. Given that Sarah and James were immune from further action following the consent decree, he'd had to lump together all the claims against them, new and old, and divide the restitution received equally among the 50 families who had lost the most.

He'd sent each of those 50 families a check for $400. I left it at that. I knew that whatever the real truth might be, Arthur himself had done the best he could.

Nothing new that would serve either to confirm or deny my suspicions of duplicity came to light in the year that followed. But all of us whom the Hagens defrauded remain convinced that the piddling amount Sarah and James were ordered to pay in restitution is proof enough that justice was somehow circumvented.

It may be that Arthur Young was forced into accepting so trifling an amount as a price for putting the Hagens once and for all out of the adoption business. From what I have been able to gather from Mike Anderson and from Arthur himself, it seems that while there is plenty of precedent in Ohio law for injunctions against engaging in unfair business practices, that law is far less clear as to whether even a person so convicted can be enjoined against conducting his business at all. By Arthur's own account, the prosecution went way out on a limb in demanding that the Hagens agree to get out of the adoption business altogether. The Hagen's attorney must have known this. For Arthur, perhaps the highest priority could not be given to those already defrauded, but to the many more who could be victims in the future.

Shutting down CAF once and for all was what mattered most. Of course, all of this is conjecture, but in retrospect, I feel he and other members of his staff did everything possible to resolve this issue fairly for the affected parties.

*   *   *

So there my story ends. But life has moved on for the people you've met here.

Scotty and Nancy McTaggart are still living in the Washington, D.C. area. Nancy is a college professor in a program to help adults with minimal educational backgrounds return to school with the hope of improving their career opportunities. Scotty works for the Maryland Cooperative Extension Service and volunteers for Habitat for Humanity. He still maintains a community-development program in Honduras that provides technical assistance to promote better, environmentally sound farming practices, and to supply water and sewage to public buildings such as hospitals. Hurricane Mitch, passing through in 1998, only increased the needs of Honduran people that much more. The work will never end for people like Scotty and Nancy.

They have two adorable little girls—both adopted, one from Guatemala and one from Honduras. The Honduran adoption, despite Scotty's connections, was fraught with delays and problems. Nothing seems to change in that respect. Worst yet, Scotty saw a picture of Sarah Hagen hanging in a ministry's office in Honduras. He said to the people there, "Don't you know that woman got in big trouble in the U.S. for deceptive practices?" They just shrugged.

Juanita remains in her beloved San Félix. The school that she founded has grown to the point of needing a full second story to accommodate the increase in students. The town has changed dramatically, too. Because it is now near the official meeting place for the Central American presidents and because of an increase in tourism, I doubt that I would recognize it. Her children are grown and now live in Guatemala City; one is a doctor, one is a lawyer, and one is a student.

Sandy and I continued to see one another for a while. We shared an interest in some of the animal projects I was working on. She has since moved on to work for a travel bureau, which gives her new opportunities to see the world, especially as her children are also grown now. I'm sure she brings happiness and humor wherever she does.

The *Dryzes* have become a wonderful family, with two boys from San Félix who have grown up in a nurturing household with Dan and Cherie. The boys, Adam* and Jesse, have kept ties with Isabella, their biological mother, and have knowledge of what goes on with their relatives back in Guatemala. The Dryzes have what amounts to the most "open adoption" I know of, despite the distances involved.

The *Partridges* rose above all the obstacles put in front of them. Not being able to help them have a family, despite my best efforts, was one of the hardest things I faced during those years. But now, they are a total success story, thanks to having adopted two beautiful children from Russia. They own their own home and are dedicated to their church and community. I knew it!

Eventually we were able to connect the *Warberg-Joneses* up with a contact in Los Angeles who worked with sources in Mexico. They adopted a fantastic little girl, with very few snags in the process. Rachel went on to law school and is now heading a large nonprofit organization and is in a position to fight the kind of injustices she had to endure.

The *Fullers* have also gone on to do wonderful things, mostly involving children's literature and educational activities with their church. This year's Christmas card pictured two children from eastern Europe and Honduras and included talk of a new home in the mountains of Tennessee.

Laverne Hopkins and I lost track of one another some years ago.

The *Cleavers*, particularly Betsy, and I have had a continuing rela-

---

* Adam has recently given me an update on his life. "I am 15 years old and can not wait to be 16. I am in my sophomore year at Barnstable High School. I play baseball a lot, football, soccer, golf, and racquetball. I am currently working at the Hyannis Christmas Tree Shops as a cashier/customer service representative/stocker. I have been there just over a year and am making good money. I play the electric guitar and maintain a spot on the Honor Roll. This summer I am hoping to take flying lessons for college requirements. After graduation, I hope to attend the United States Air Force Academy and attain my degree in aeronautical engineering while flying for the Air Force, and maybe join the Space Program. I consider myself athletic and popular. At the time I don't have a girlfriend but have caught the eyes of several young ladies. I enjoy hanging out with friends, playing any sports, lifting weights at the gym, and playing the guitar."

tionship, albeit long distance. Following the CAF disaster, they pursued adoption in their own area. Unfortunately, these efforts were fraught with complications and problems. I think the Cleavers probably endured the worst that social services can dispense. Many times only their strong faith in God, and the belief that what goes around comes around, carried them through. To their credit, there is no bitterness. Today, they have five children, including two who were adopted domestically, and are in the process of moving to a larger house.

The *Lords* now live outside of Springfield. They have a wonderful life. As well-educated professionals, they bring a wealth of cultural activity to the lives of their two children. They travel and live abroad a lot.

My old friend, *Lucinda*, has not had an easy life. Since I last saw her, a debilitating illness has left her unable to work, drive, or socialize; she can barely even care for herself. Then came a divorce and a move to a different locale. We still reminisce when we talk, usually by phone, and I feel guilty telling her the good things that have happened in my life. She gave me so much 15 years ago—support, humor, and spirituality. I will always be in her debt.

As for *myself*, after the disheartening experience in the Philippines I began to think of alternative ways to do good in this world, and I decided to explore the idea of creating a wildlife-rehabilitation center. Animals brought with them a lot fewer problems than did people. Animals also required a less intense level of emotional commitment that might be easier to reconcile with my role as mother to a still-small child. I even had a name for the organization that was taking shape in my mind. I would call it Orenda. "Orenda" is a Seneca Indian word that means "protected place." I liked that. So I shifted gears and threw my energies into creating the Orenda Wildlife Trust. I endowed a small rehabilitation facility in West Barnstable, Massachusetts, helped to organize a network of volunteers to staff it, and set about soliciting donations from local landowners of open space to be preserved as "protected places."

The Trust has developed nicely on its own, and I have been able to step back and act only as an occassional advisor. The rehabilitation program was turned over to the Humane Society of the United States and is now a first-rate wildlife hospital and training center. I have become increasingly active in animal-rights issues and in programs dealing with wildlife and companion-animal issues all over the world.

Dave is still working with boats and has designed his own multi-use Speedwell skiff. Chris and Karen have grown up to be busy and wonderfully caring people and both living close enough to us that we see them often. Tammy will be a junior in high school. She relates with both adults and her own age group, but is very much a typical teenager. Her main loves are music and her friends.

Now, in quiet moments, when I look into the wide, expressive face of my 16-year-old daughter, I see all of Central America, with its joys and tragedies, its beauty and its devastation. I see generations of solid Indian peoples visited and conquered by various peoples from an ocean away. And I see determination to endure all this and survive.

The sounds come back too. The catchiness of the marimba bands, the haunting sound of the flute, the banter and bustle of the open markets. Once again I can smell the odor of countless piles of wood burning in hundreds of little homes for cooking and warmth. There was always a smokiness in the air. And the air itself was special: hot and humid in the valleys, cooler in the mountains, but seldom windy. Early afternoon always made me feel groggy, no matter where I was.

I still remember what it was like when I first looked down from the plane at El Salvador. My mind was absorbed by the height and lushness of the mountains—green often extending to the brilliant white sands of the coast. So undeveloped and beautiful. The dirt roads, hundreds of tiny threads wrapped around the mountains, tracing back again and finally disappearing out of sight. If I could have looked closer I would have seen *campesinos* carrying everyday pieces of their existence from place to place. It seemed so peaceful—so forever.

But, of course, I knew this was not a tranquil place, because otherwise I would have no reason to be on that plane. Long years of poverty and civil violence had taken their toll on that countryside, and many families had been destroyed—either physically or emotionally. And I, like others, was there to do what? Reap advantage of a tragic situation, or help by taking away some part of this culture to be raised in safer, better-nourished surroundings?

As the years roll on, I realize that these little transplants bring a lot of their own heritage with them: the pride, the stubbornness, the high energy, and the ability to show love in open ways. My husband and I often joke that, with enough protein, Central America could soon take over the world.

During the years I was involved in the world of international adoptions, I came to care deeply about the land and its peoples, especially the Indians, and I learned to resent the military presence. I never got over teenagers walking around with machine guns. What a waste! Give them a shovel and some plants or materials to start a school so they could restore their beautiful homeland.

There is a glimmer of hope, however. The Federation of Central American States now has meetings close to where the boundaries of Guatemala, El Salvador, and Honduras meet, a place where I remember seeing tanks and military outposts. They come to talk of common problems—economics, peace and relationships with big world powers. They come to address their countries' concerns as only they can do. Uncle Sam, please step aside, thank you, unless you are really there to help. Perhaps the most promising new development for the entire region was the publication in February 1999 of a truth commission's report cataloging the horrible toll of the three decades of civil war in Guatemala and the subsequent apology by President Clinton for the United States' misguided policy of support for the military.

$$* \quad * \quad *$$

You may well wonder what drove me to take on all this in the first place. Surely I could see early on that it wasn't going to be an easy road. Was I crazy, stupid, or what? Frankly, I never could have imagined all that I would encounter doing what I naively perceived was the right thing. I now realize that I was venturing into some rather new territory, and the people who worked with me got carried along into it. Certainly there were no road maps or guidelines to follow.

When I recently saw the movie *Cider House Rules,* I was struck by the fact that in the United States, not so long ago, *domestic* adoption was a sad and unregulated process. Many children were never given the chance to have a family. Of course, much of that has changed in the last 50 years due to progressive attitudes and new laws about the rights and needs of children. Now many children available for adoption in this country find permanent homes. It should be noted, however, that tragically some children even here in the United States still don't find lasting homes. For example, the most recent report by the Massachusetts Adoption Resources Exchange, Inc. notes that they list 338 children waiting for adoptive homes. Most of these are children of color and/or sibling groups. Currently they list 200 families looking to adopt, 31 of whom are families of color and 169 of whom are Caucasian.

Many Third World countries present an extreme perspective as they are still in the dark ages regarding children's rights. Certainly the world I stepped into was one of the least regulated and most unmanageable one could imagine. I guess I can take heart in the fact that while I made many mistakes and suffered considerable despair along that journey, I have seen the wonderful lives that children can have by being adopted. That realization makes it all worthwhile.

Fortunately, we have reason to be optimist that adoption conditions for children in the developing world will improve. The reason is the Hague Convention on International Adoption, the multilateral treaty that was drafted with the participation of 66 nations in 1993. The Convention has created a legal framework for all adoptions between countries that become parties to it. When fully ratified, it will facilitate real change in the way international adoptions are addressed by most governments. It will create an opportunity to tear down the walls of senseless bureaucratic requirements, to establish standard rules and regulations for the way all adoptions are carried out, and to promote trust and equity among countries, agencies, and those who wish to adopt. As of August 2000 a total of 29 countries have ratified the terms of the Hague Convention. The United States has still not taken the all important step of getting congressional approval of enabling legislation. Congressman Bill Delahunt, of my own district in Massachusetts and an adoptive parent, has sponsored a bill (H.R. 2909) specifically for that purpose and that bill has been passed by the House of Representatives. An amended version of the bill was later passed by the

Senate, and now it is up to the two chambers to resolve the differences. Since the legislation has already been scrutinized by adoption experts I am confident that a bill will emerge that will preserve the interests of the Hague Convention. I sincerely hope that it passes quickly to help ensure that stories like mine will no longer be common.

Epilogue

WHEN I set out to tell this story, my goal was to help others who were thinking about venturing down the path of international adoption. I wanted to alert them to the pitfalls and prepare them for the emotional roller-coaster ride they were likely to encounter.

But in writing my cautionary tale, I'm afraid I may have painted too discouraging a picture. Some people may be scared away. I hope not. No one believes more strongly in international adoptions than I do. The vast majority of them are totally successful. They offer a rare opportunity to step beyond the normal American lifestyle, to learn from the values of other cultures. Each successfully adopted child is the whole story of people moving heaven and earth for the benefit and love of a single child. And for the parents and kids, it is totally worthwhile. They have the opportunity to know a unique history, shared by few and as powerful as any bond can be.

International adoption is not for everyone. If you are committed—and commitment is critical—you must do your homework. Read books, attend conferences and seminars, and learn as much as you can. Join support groups for families adopting children and those who have already adopted. To help get you started on your research, I have included an appendix that lists selected organizations, books, and websites.

The single most important decision you will make is the selection of the right people to help you find a child overseas. Given the complexity of the process, the distances, the strange cultures, and the unfamiliar political systems, you have to rely on someone else's expertise. Usually this will be an adoption agency, but you should keep your eyes open for freelance individuals who are well qualified to provide the support you need.*

When you screen candidates, I recommend you concentrate on three vital elements: *experience, integrity,* and *resourcefulness.* You need an agency (or a person) that has been operating in the field for some time, that has made mistakes and learned from them. It should know the adoption process generally but have a solid track record in the country where it will be looking for your child. Lack of experience was the principal weakness of Hermandad de Guadalupe. I sometimes cringe when I remember our naiveté in those early days.

As for integrity, you want to select an agency that has high standards, has a stake in doing well, and is willing to go the extra mile to make sure that your adoption is successful. This is the quality that saved Hermandad. We were as determined as our clients that we deliver on our promises.

You should also look for an agency (or a person) that is resourceful in solving problems and in finding adoptable children. Some agencies just seem to get lazy or become overly conservative.

It is difficult to assess an agency's qualifications before developing a working relationship. The best approach is to talk with other families who have adopted children through the same organization. Speak with them in confidence about the agency. If management is reluctant to make those referrals, you have a sure sign the agency is not for you.

Another suggestion is to ask the agency a barrage of questions, probing into each of the problem areas described in this book. If you get a sense that management downplays the difficulties and implies that the process is simple, you may be talking to the wrong people.

---

* A licensed agency must perform the home study and follow-up evaluation, but independent persons can manage all other steps in the adoption process.

You should be sure to check out a prospective agency with the appropriate authorities: the licensing board of the agency's state and the consumer complaints unit of the attorney general's office of both the agency's state and your own. In addition to helping screen the agency, they can advise you about the regulations and laws in place to protect adoptive parents against the sorts of disappointments and financial losses described in this book.

The other major task you have to accomplish is to put yourself in the right frame of mind. *Keep your standards high but expectations low.* When troubles arise, you will be better able to accept them and roll with the punches. If problems don't appear, then count yourself lucky. *Be flexible.* Give up preconceived notions if they don't appear realistic. *Be patient.* Don't jump on a plane too quickly—that is, unless you like adventure and have an especially tough constitution that can withstand disappointment. There will be another opportunity. Unfortunately, there are many children who would make wonderful adoptees. If you miss a chance, say to yourself, "Well, it probably wasn't meant to be," and be thankful that some other parent has given that child a much-needed home. Then continue your search.

Selected Resources

The following is a partial list of resources—books, organizations, and websites—that may be helpful to people who want to get more information about the adoption process, both international and domestic. In assembling the list, we have not attempted to be comprehensive, and we recognize there are many worthy sources we have failed to include. Their omission in no way reflects our evaluation of them. The brief descriptions of the books are derived from information provided by the publishers or readers. We do not vouch for their accuracy. We have not included resources devoted to specific topics within the adoption field (e.g., open adoption, health issues) or to geographic regions.

BOOKS

International Adoption

"Are These Kids Yours?": American Families with Children Adopted from Other Countries by Cherie Register. Free Press, 1990; 240 pages.

Directed mainly at helping families deal with the unique challenges associated with adopting a child from another culture.

How to Adopt Internationally: A Guide to Agency-Directed and Independent Adoptions by Heino R. Erichsen and Jean Nelson-Erichsen. Mesa House Publishing, 1997; 280 pages.

A book organized around 23 steps, covering all parts of the international adoption process. It includes a "Compendium" of information concerning the individual child-placing countries.

International Adoption: Sensitive Advice for Prospective Parents
by Jean Knoll. Chicago Review Press, 1994; 198 pages.

A personal account written from the perspective of a single mother trying to adopt a child overseas and providing advice to prospective parents.

The International Adoption Handbook: How to Make an Overseas Adoption Work for You by Myra Alperson. Henry Holt, 1997; 224 pages.

A detailed guide to the adoption process, with descriptions of experiences of parents who have adopted from other countries.

With Eyes Wide Open: A Workbook for Parents Adopting International Children Over Age One by Margi Miller and Nancy Ward. Children's Home Society of Minnesota, 1996; 155 pages.

Designed to help adoptive parents prepare themselves for bringing into their family a child with life experiences.

General Adoption

The Adoption Option: Complete Handbook, 2000–2001 by Christine Adamec. Prima Publishing, 1999; 640 pages.

A comprehensive guide to adoption resources in the United States and abroad, in addition to essays on specific concerns of parents.

The Adoption Resource Book by Lois Gilman. Harper Reference, 1998 (4th ed.); 576 pages.

A large book covering a full assortment of issues concerning the adoption process, including words of advice and caution.

The Complete Adoption Book by Laura Beauvais-Godwin. Adams Media Corporation, 1997; 496 pages.

A resource that discusses the adoption process from beginning to end.

How to Make Adoption an Affordable Option The Child Welfare League of America, 1997; 76 pages.

Examines the range of expenses typically incurred by persons adopting a child within the U.S. or from other countries; cites sources for financial assistance.

ADOPTION-RELATED ORGANIZATIONS

International Concerns for Children (ICC)

911 Cypress Drive, Boulder, CO 80303-2821

(303) 494-8333

icc@boulder.net

http://www.iccadopt.org

Started in 1979, ICC works to provide prospective parents with up-to-date facts on "waiting children" and their countries of origin. It publishes annually, with monthly updates, the *Report on Intercountry Adoption,* which details costs, waiting periods, and names of agencies, among other items.

Joint Council on International Children's Services (JCICS)

1320 19th Street, NW, Suite 200, Washington DC 20036

(202) 429-0400

http://www.jcics.org

The oldest and largest organization of licensed nonprofit international adoption agencies in the world. It seeks to find ways to make international adoption, when appropriate, as rational and ethical as possible. Its website has updates on adoption legislation.

National Adoption Information Clearinghouse (NAIC)

330 C Street, SW, Washington, DC 20447

(703) 352-3488   (888) 251-0075

naic@calib.com

http://www.calib.com/naic

An organization founded in 1986 by the U.S. Congress to provide easily accessible information on a wide-ranging scope of adoption issues, both international and domestic. Much of it, including databases of support groups, agencies, and state specialists, is on its website.

National Council for Adoption

1930 17th Street, NW

Washington, DC 20009-6207

(202) 328-8072

ncfa@ncfa-usa.org

http://www.ncfa-usa.org

A membership organization that is a source for much information, advice, and support on adoption.

North American Council on Adoptable Children

970 Raymond Avenue, Suite 106
St. Paul, MN 55114-1149
(651) 644-3036
info@nacac.org
http://www.nacac.org

Conducts a broad range of programs, such as education, parent support, research, and advocacy to monitor and improve adoption systems, including international adoption.

Open Door Society of Massachusetts, Inc.

1750 Washington Street
Holliston, MA 01746-2234
(508) 429-4260   (800) 93-adopt
odsma@odsma.org
http://www.odsma.org

Despite its name, this organization operates without geographic restrictions, providing assistance, information, and advocacy for all people concerned with adoption issues.

WEBSITES

As regular users of the Internet are aware, one must be cautious in selecting the information on which to rely. When browsing under the topic of international adoption, one needs to apply the same high standards to websites as one does to adoption agencies.

Independent

http://www.adoption.about.com

http://www.adopting.org

http://www.adopting.com

Three sites that address the issue of adoption as a whole. Each has many links to organizations, individuals, and articles.

http://www.tapestrybooks.com

The place to go when looking for books on specific aspects of adoption, including children's books.

http://www.adoptkorea.com

Despite its country-specific address, this website provides well-organized information, advice, and links useful to anyone contemplating an international adoption.

Governmental

http://travel.state.gov/adopt.html

http//travel.state.gov/children's_issues.html

Two sites with valuable information on international adoption as seen from the perspective of the U.S. State Department.